Surviving
The San Francisco
EARTHQUAKE

By Jo Cleland
Illustrated By Pete McDonnell

ROURKE PUBLISHING

Vero Beach, Florida 32964

JFS
Graphic

www.rourkepublishing.com

PHOTO CREDITS: © AlexMax: Title page, pages 4, 26, 27, 28, 29, 30, 31, 32;
© Library of Congress: pages 4, 5, 26, 27, 28; © Andrea Danti: page 29

Edited by Katherine M. Thal
Illustrated by Pete McDonnell
Art Direction and Page Layout by Renee Brady

Library of Congress Cataloging-in-Publication Data

Cleland, Joann.
Surviving the San Francisco Earthquake / Jo Cleland.
    p. cm. -- (Eye on history graphic illustrated)
Includes bibliographical references and index.
ISBN 978-1-60694-439-4 (alk. paper)
ISBN 978-1-60694-548-3 (soft cover)
1. San Francisco Earthquake and Fire, Calif., 1906--Juvenile literature. 2. Earthquakes--California--San Francisco--History--20th century--Juvenile literature. 3. Fires--California--San Francisco--History--20th century--Juvenile literature. 4. San Francisco (Calif.)--History--20th century--Juvenile literature. 5. Graphic novels. I. Title.
F869.S357C55 2010
979.4'61051--dc22
                                2009020500

Printed in the USA
CG/CG

www.rourkepublishing.com - rourke@rourkepublishing.com
Post Office Box 643328 Vero Beach, Florida 32964

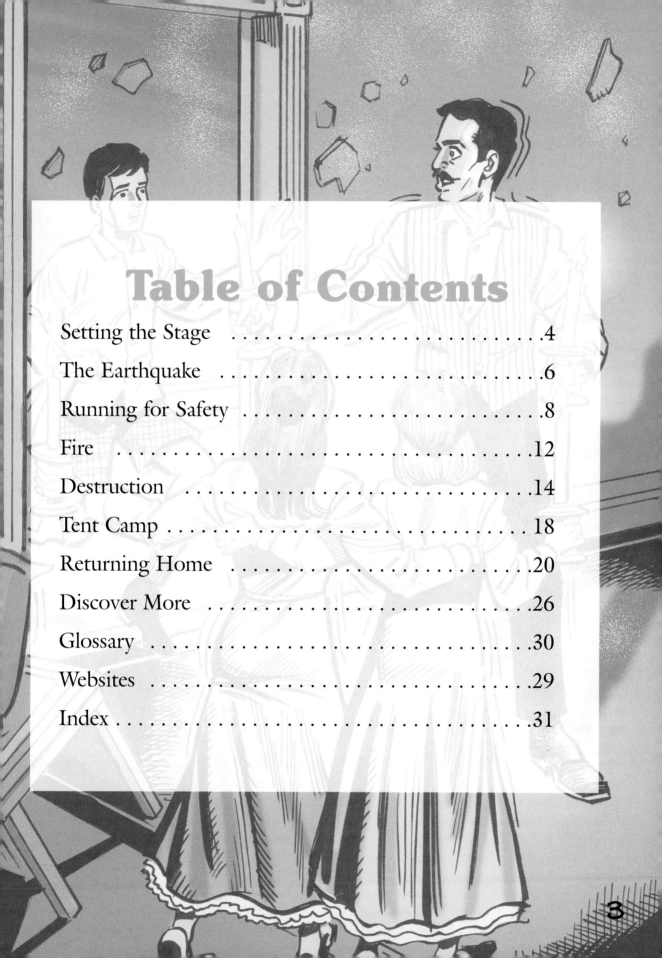

Table of Contents

Setting the Stage 4

The Earthquake 6

Running for Safety 8

Fire 12

Destruction 14

Tent Camp 18

Returning Home 20

Discover More 26

Glossary 30

Websites 29

Index 31

The San Francisco News

Tuesday

Issue 7   Volume 11

April 24, 1906

City Suffered Enormous Loss from Quake and Fires

While last Wednesday's earthquake caused buildings to collapse and people to flee across open cracks in the ground, greater damage came from the fires that followed. The quake lasted only two minutes, but fires raged for three days. Flames reached a mile high into the sky. Thousands of people have escaped and have been housed in a tent city built for those who have been left stranded and homeless. Others scrambled onto ferryboats that took them to safety. It is estimated that 3,000 acres of the city have been flattened, and that at least 500 people have died. Today, those who have survived and remain here are in shock over the devastation.

Many of the buildings on the cross street of Post and Grant Avenues in San Francisco were destroyed in the earthquake. Fires added to the destruction of the city as well.

On April 18, 1906 at 5:12 in the morning, an earthquake shook the city of San Francisco, California. Witnesses describe the ground as moving like an angry ocean during the quake, with a waving and buckling motion that caused many of the city's buildings to shake and fall apart. The quake also caused several fires to break out and spread, destroying much of the city. The force of the earthquake was felt all along the California coast and even into the neighboring states of Nevada and Oregon.

The Earthquake

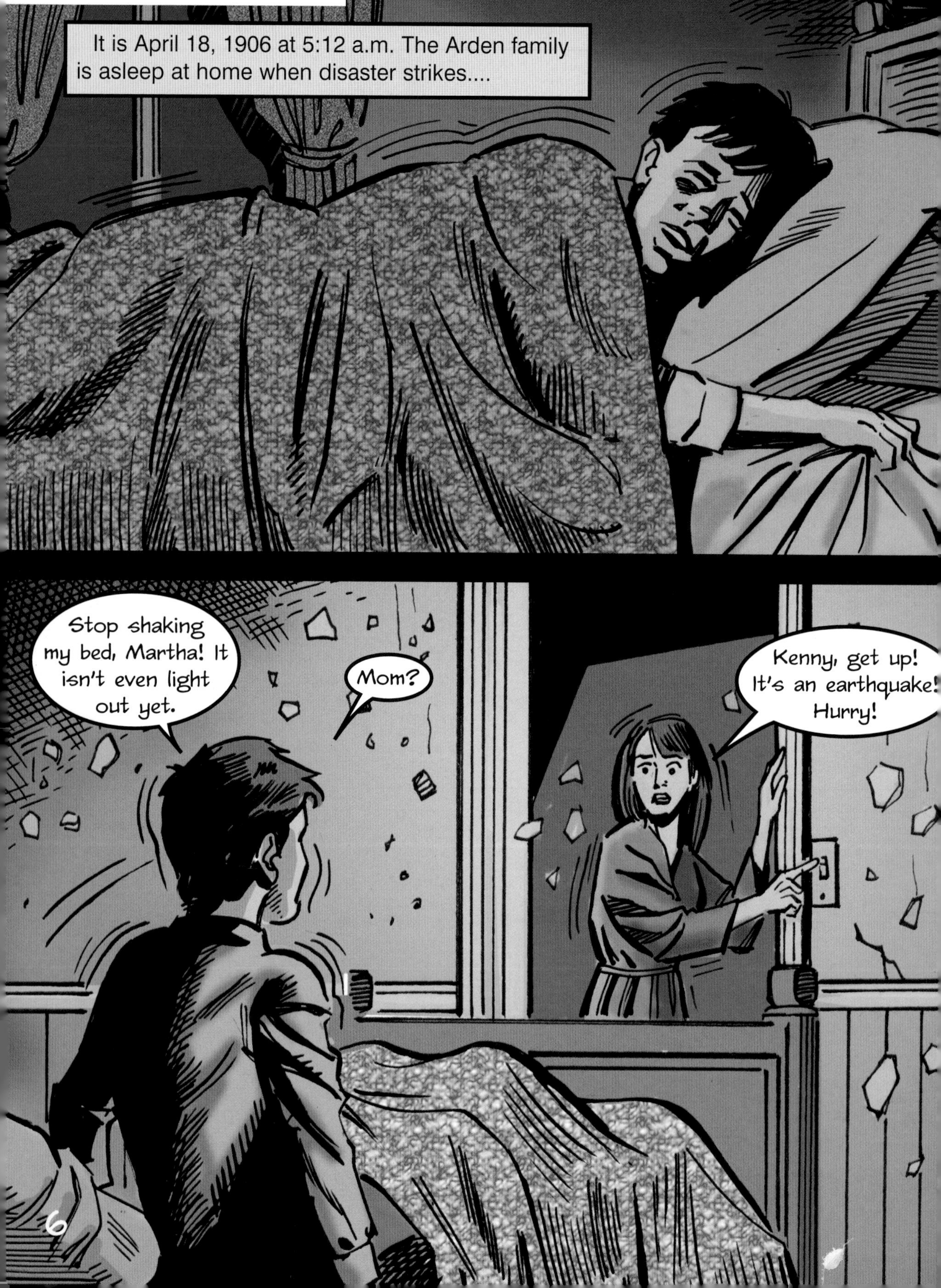

It is April 18, 1906 at 5:12 a.m. The Arden family is asleep at home when disaster strikes....
Stop shaking my bed, Martha! It isn't even light out yet.
Mom?
Kenny, get up! It's an earthquake! Hurry!

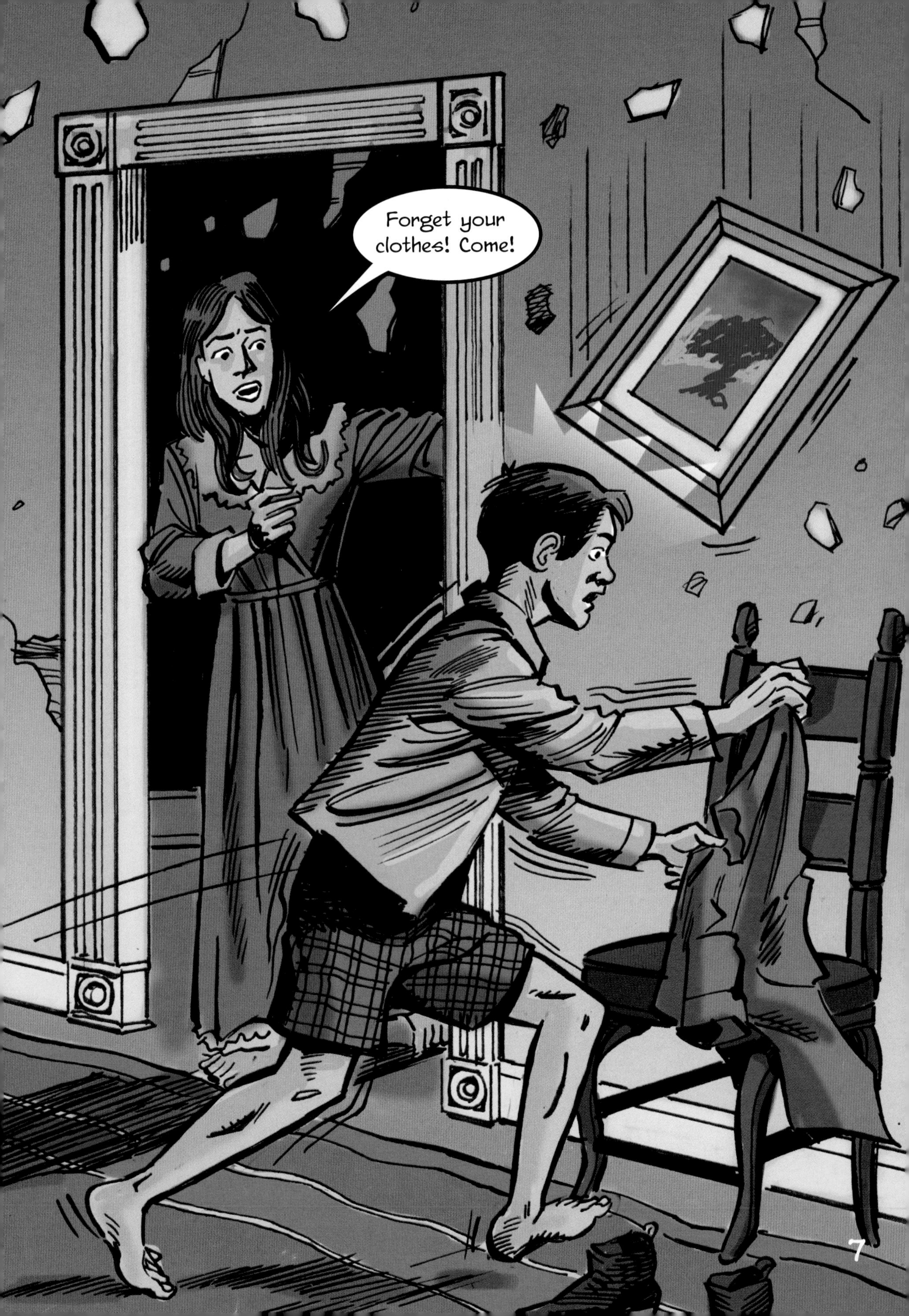
Forget your clothes! Come!

Running for Safety

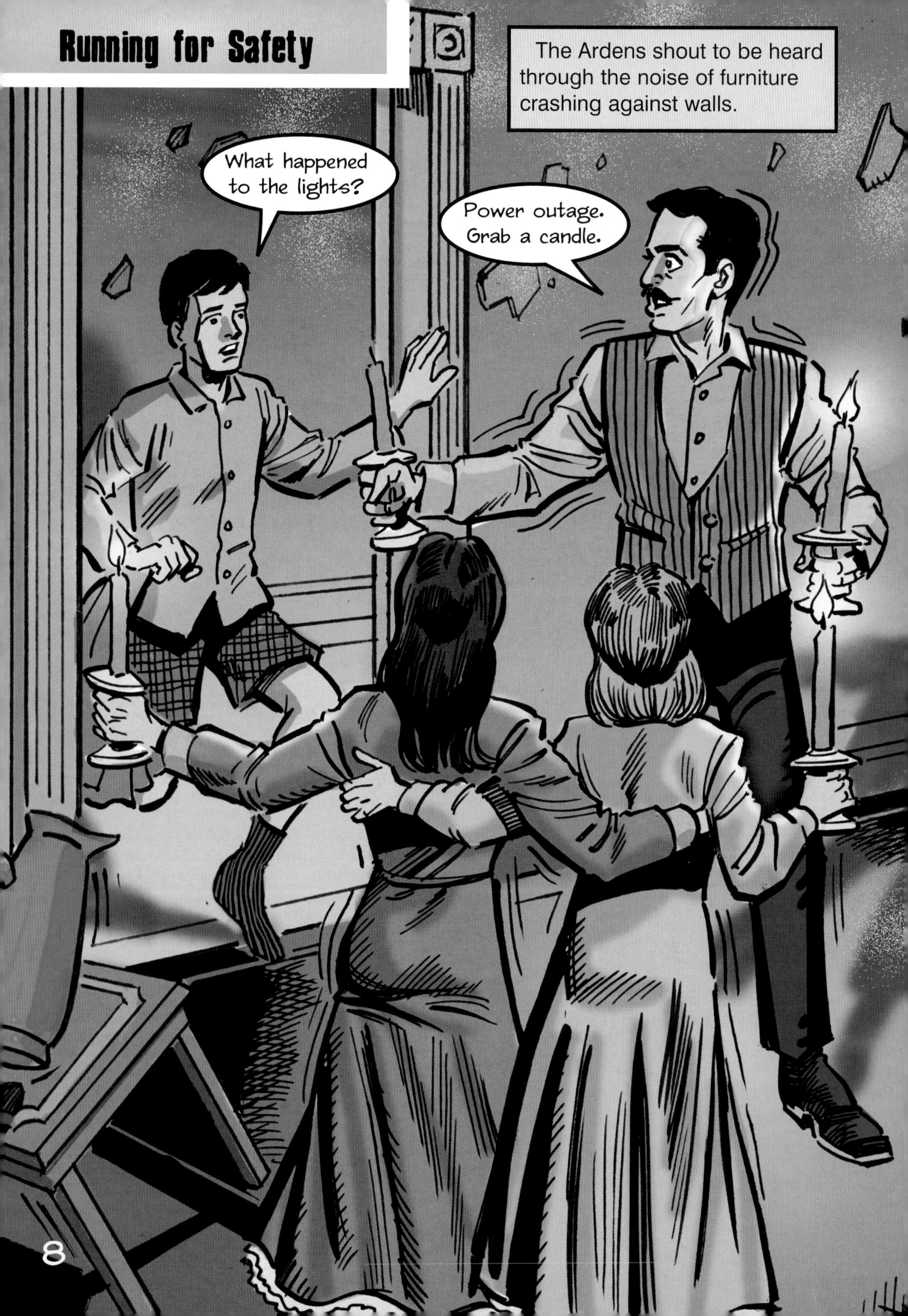
The Ardens shout to be heard through the noise of furniture crashing against walls.
What happened to the lights?
Power outage. Grab a candle.

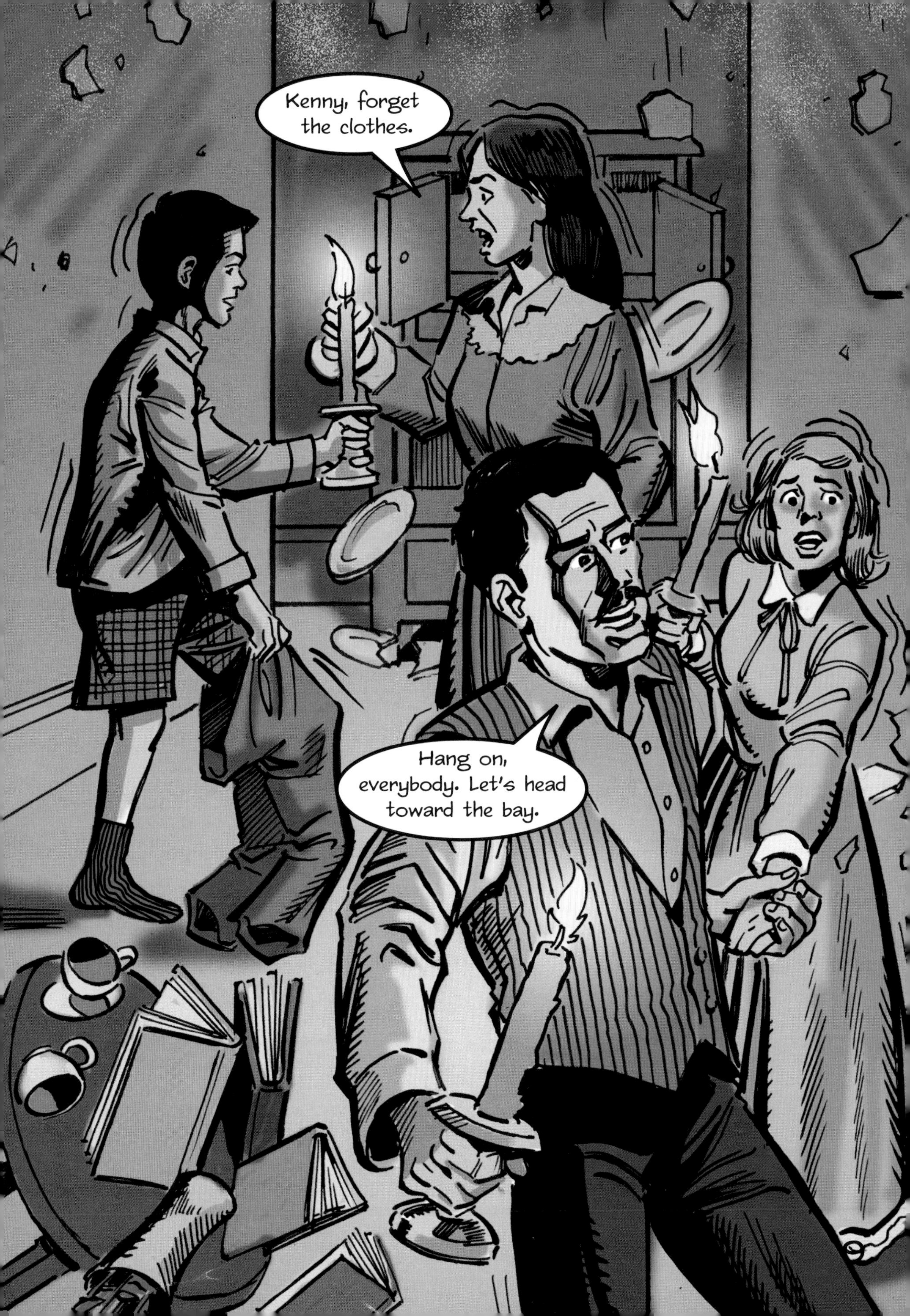
Kenny, forget the clothes.
Hang on, everybody. Let's head toward the bay.

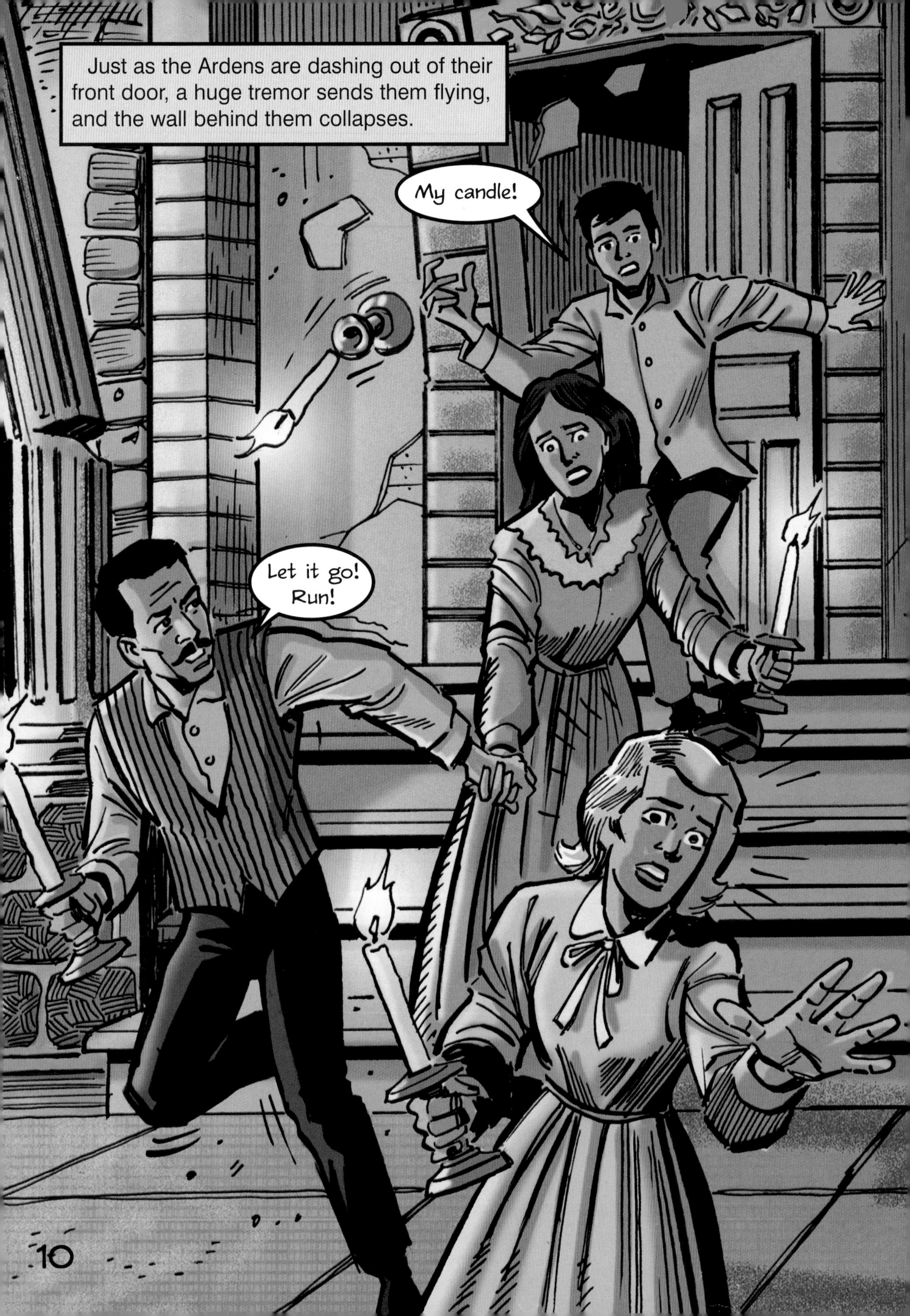
Just as the Ardens are dashing out of their front door, a huge tremor sends them flying, and the wall behind them collapses.
My candle!
Let it go! Run!

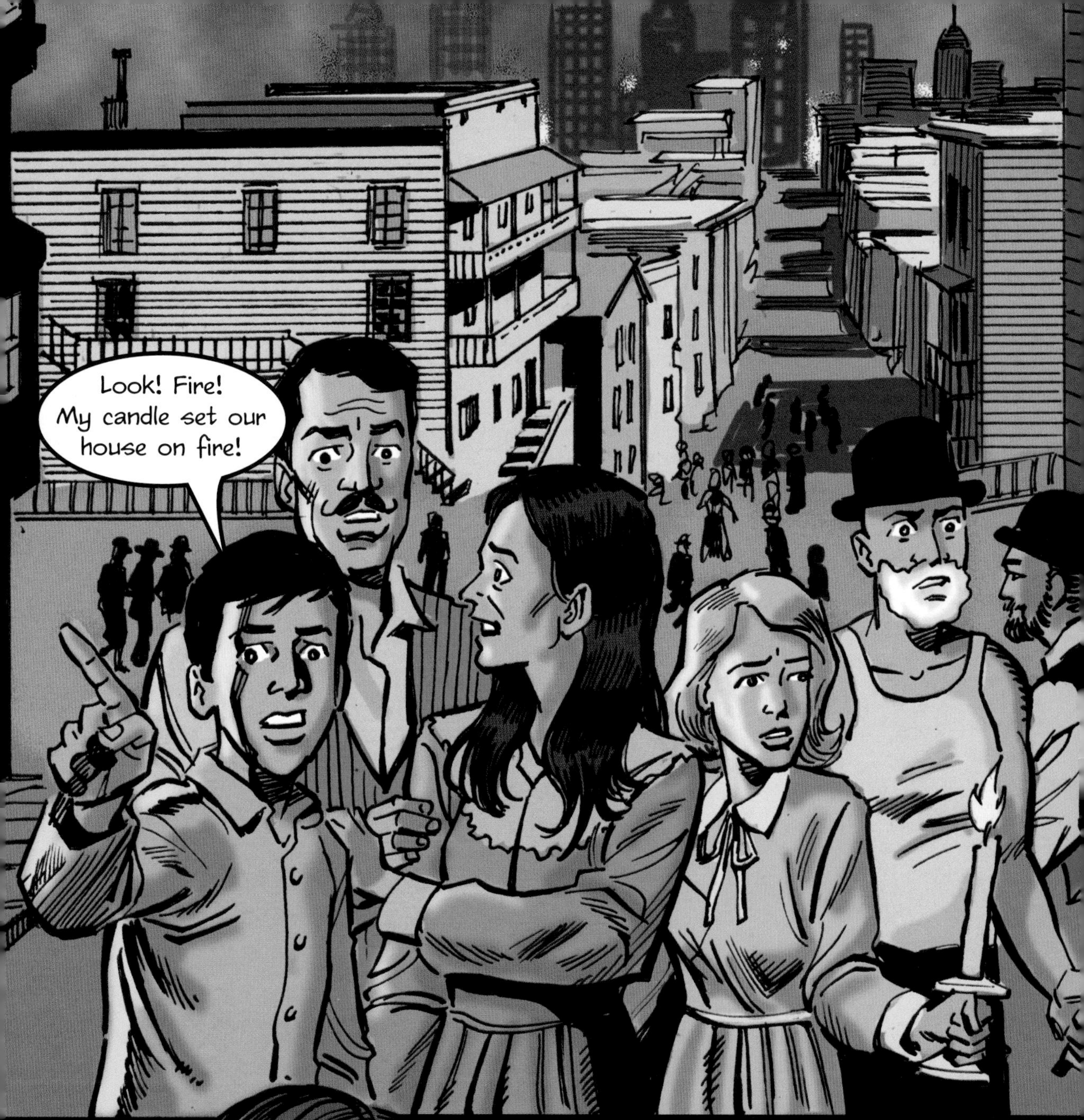
Look! Fire! My candle set our house on fire!

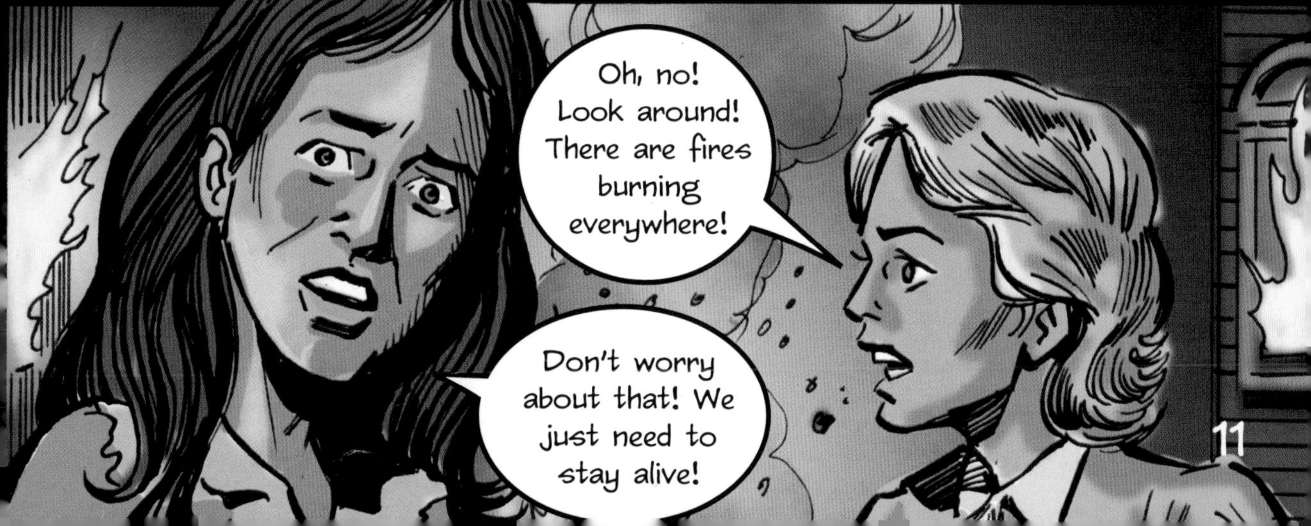
Oh, no! Look around! There are fires burning everywhere!
Don't worry about that! We just need to stay alive!

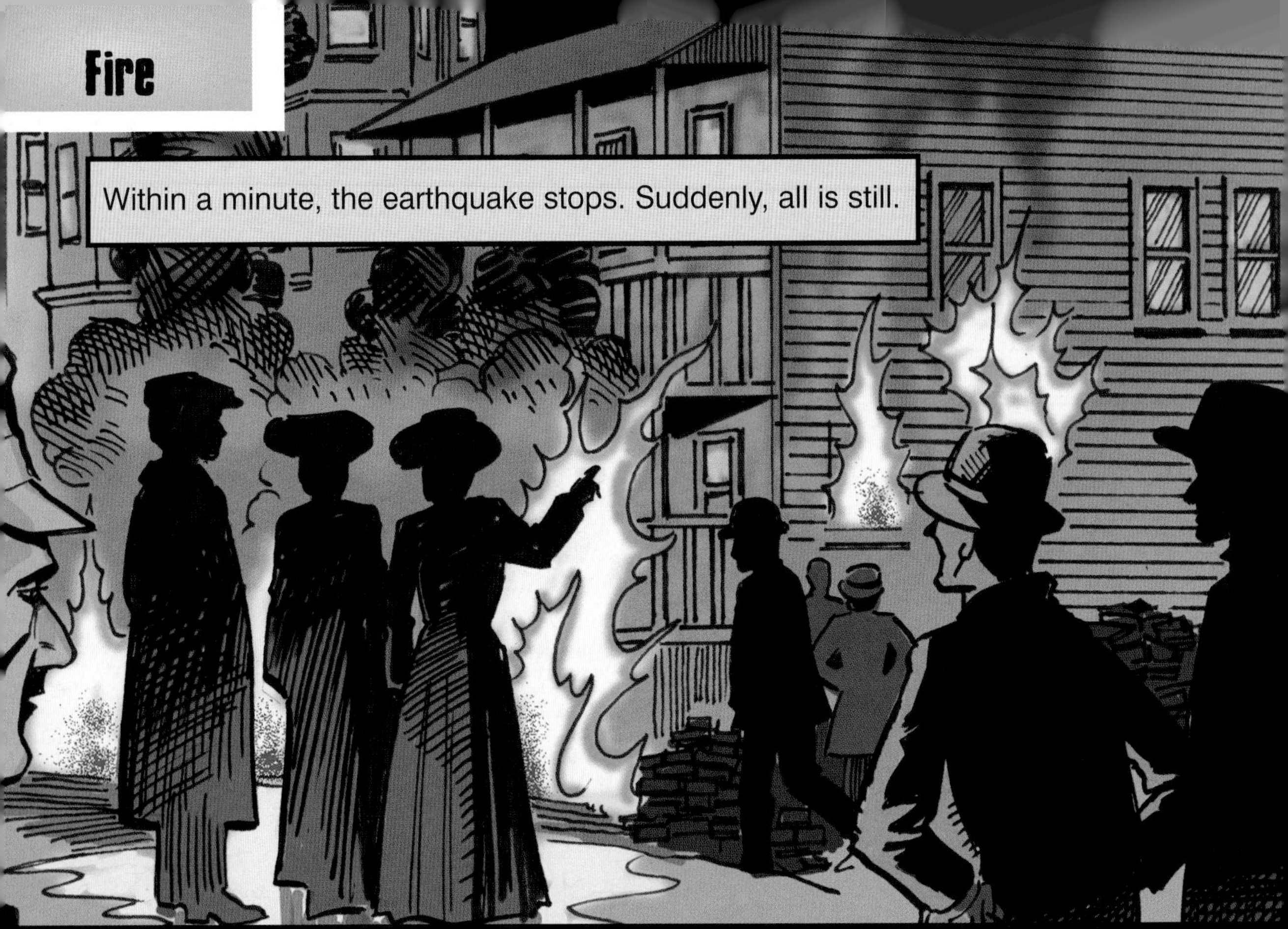
Within a minute, the earthquake stops. Suddenly, all is still.

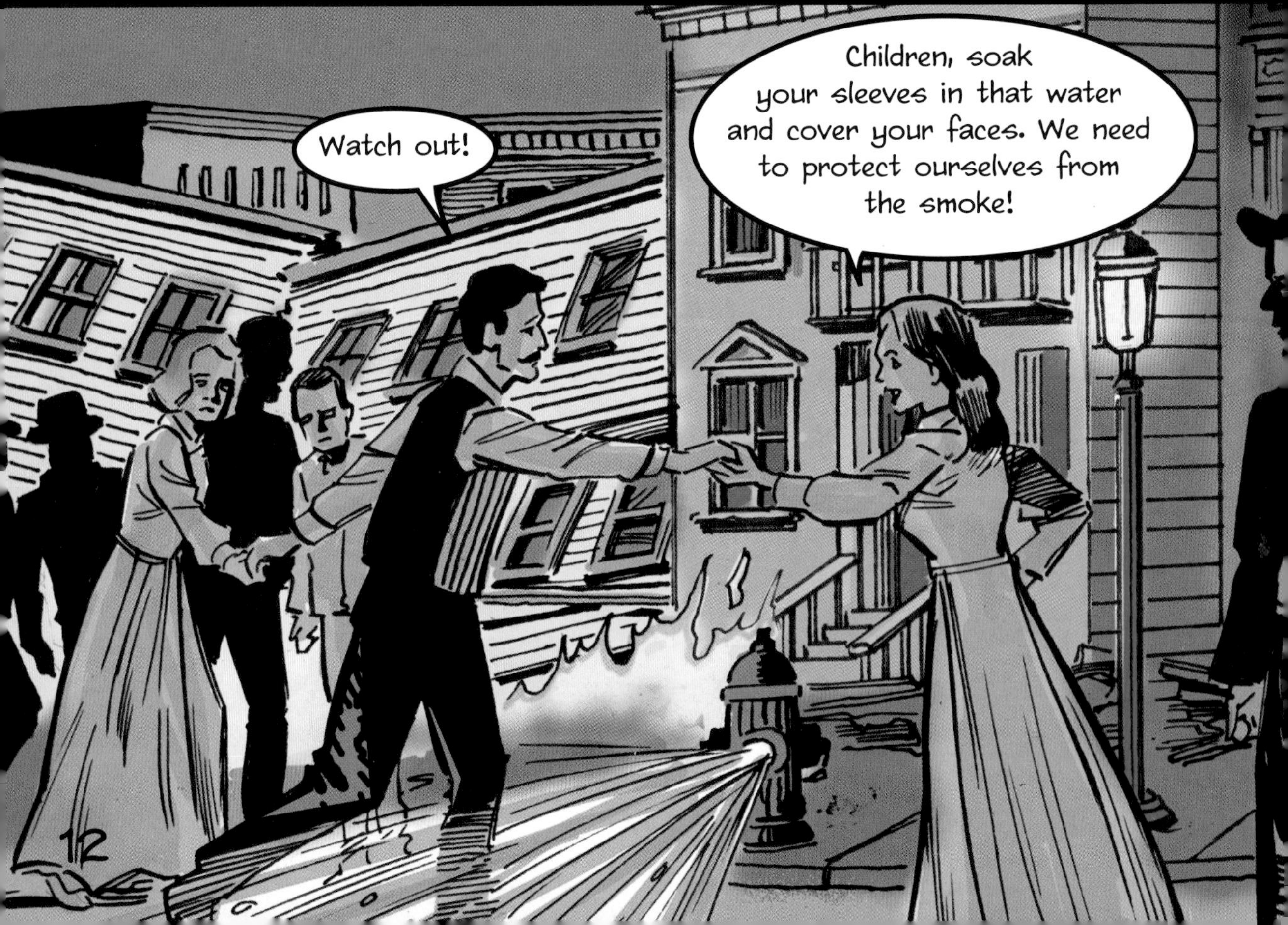
Watch out!
Children, soak your sleeves in that water and cover your faces. We need to protect ourselves from the smoke!

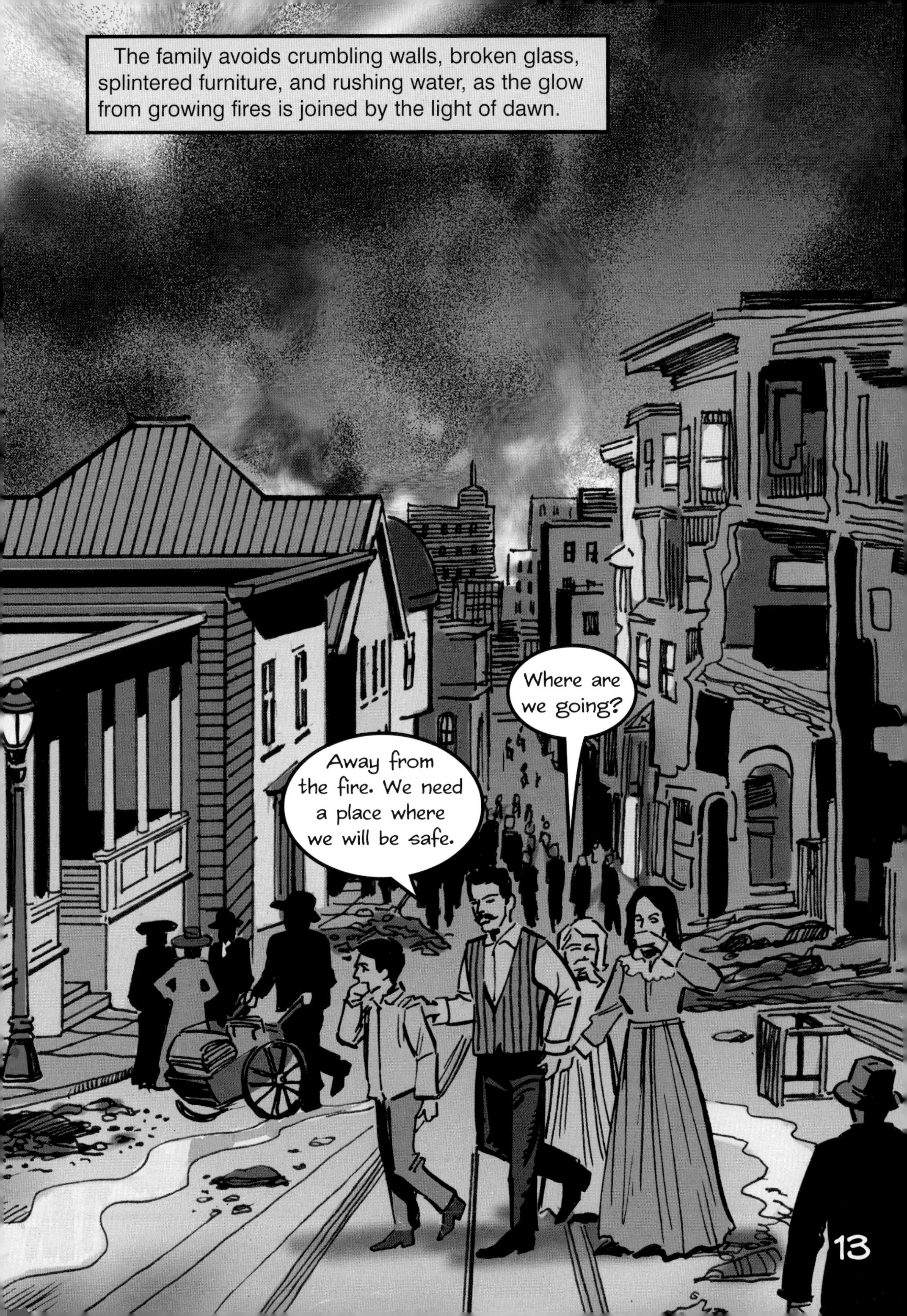
The family avoids crumbling walls, broken glass, splintered furniture, and rushing water, as the glow from growing fires is joined by the light of dawn.
Where are we going?
Away from the fire. We need a place where we will be safe.

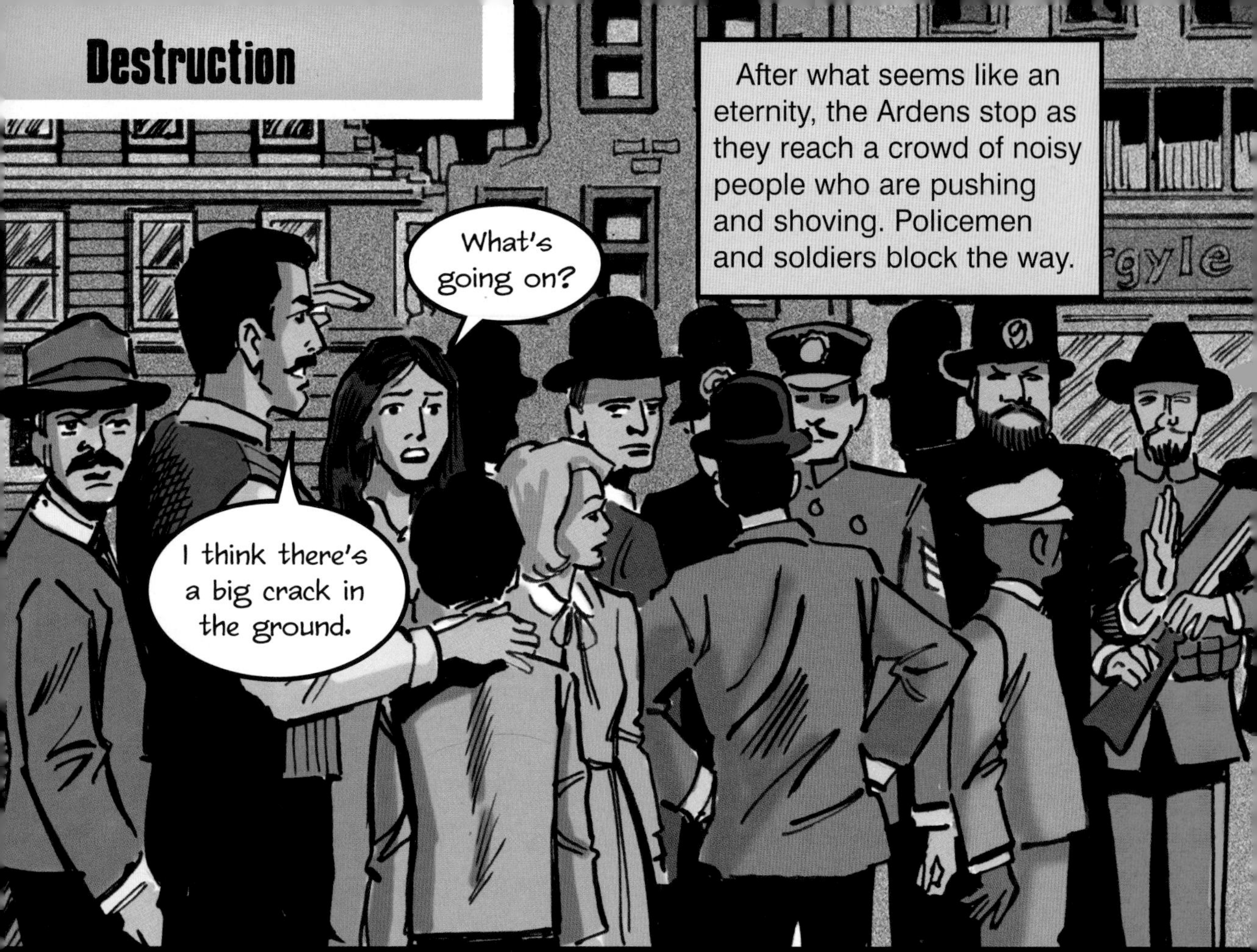
After what seems like an eternity, the Ardens stop as they reach a crowd of noisy people who are pushing and shoving. Policemen and soldiers block the way.
What's going on?
I think there's a big crack in the ground.

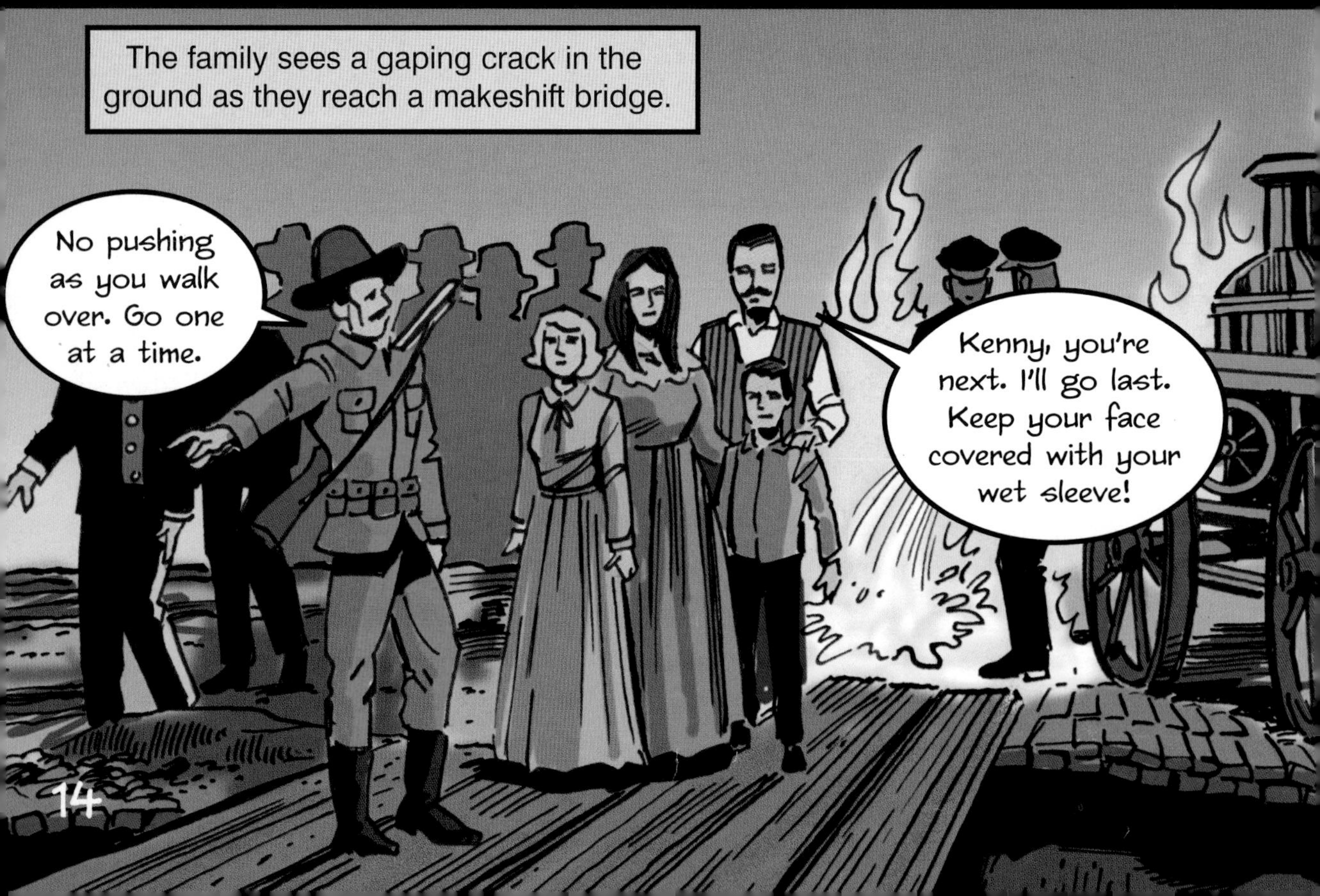
The family sees a gaping crack in the ground as they reach a makeshift bridge.
No pushing as you walk over. Go one at a time.
Kenny, you're next. I'll go last. Keep your face covered with your wet sleeve!

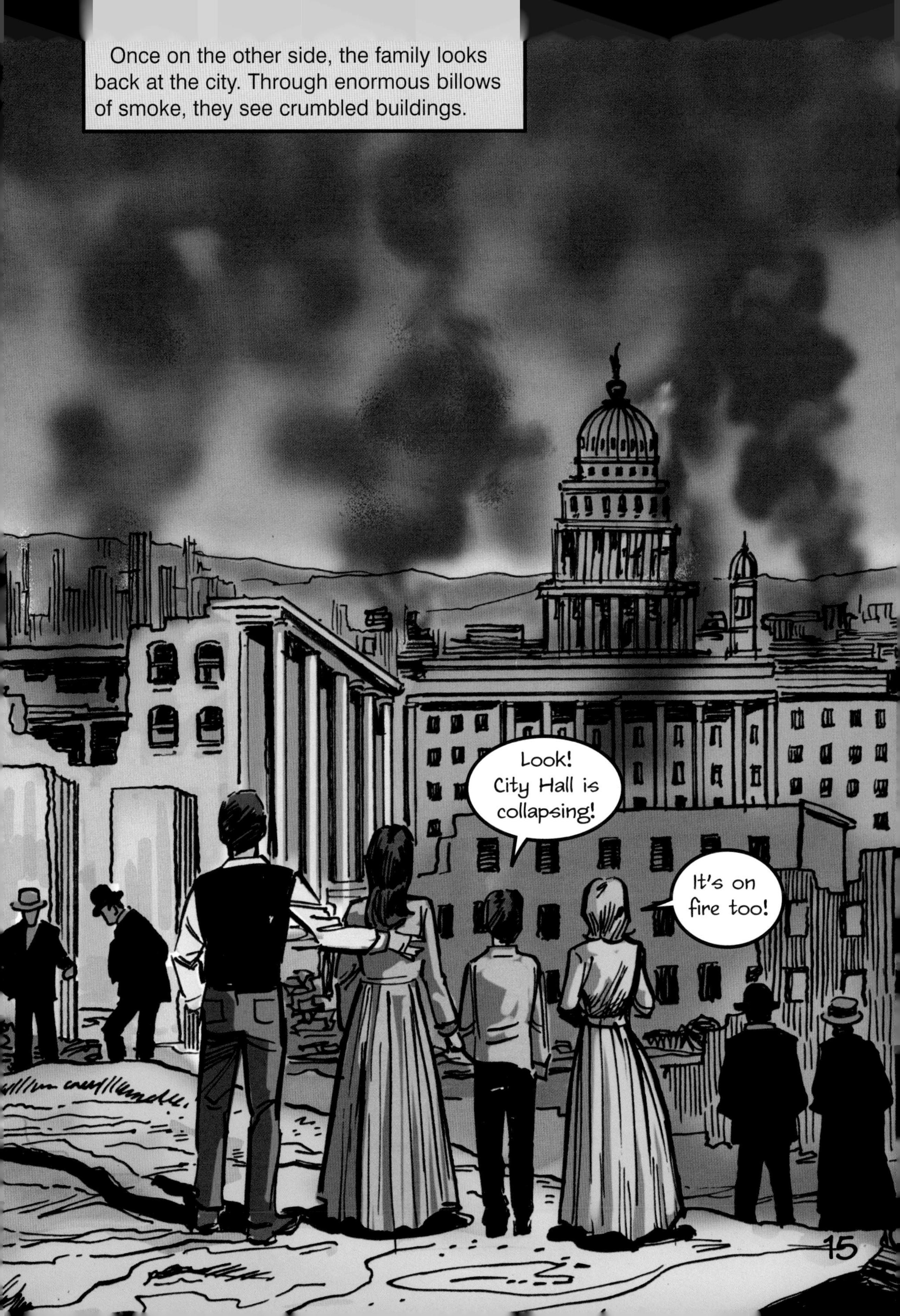
Once on the other side, the family looks back at the city. Through enormous billows of smoke, they see crumbled buildings.
Look! City Hall is collapsing!
It's on fire too!

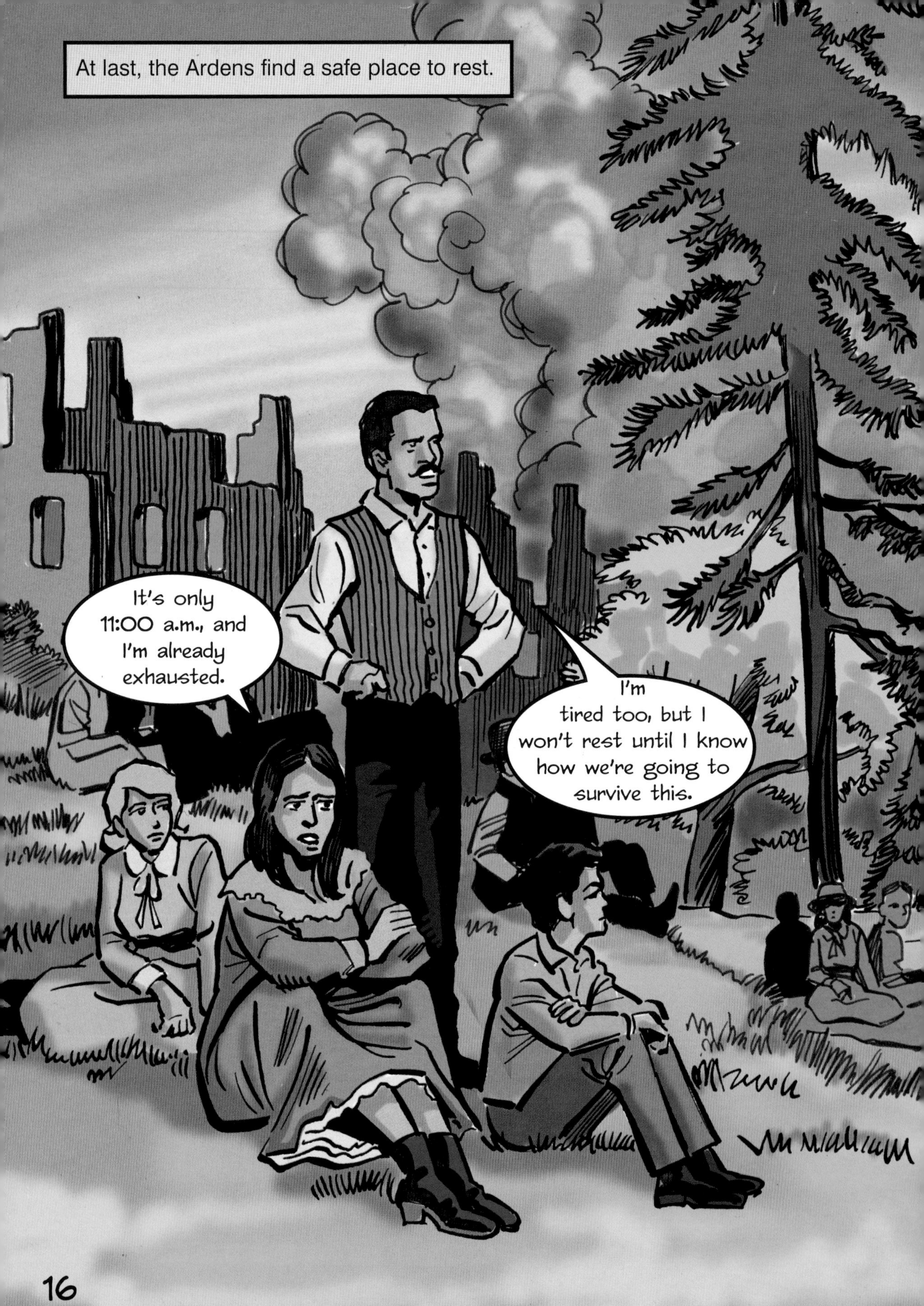
At last, the Ardens find a safe place to rest.
It's only 11:00 a.m., and I'm already exhausted.
I'm tired too, but I won't rest until I know how we're going to survive this.

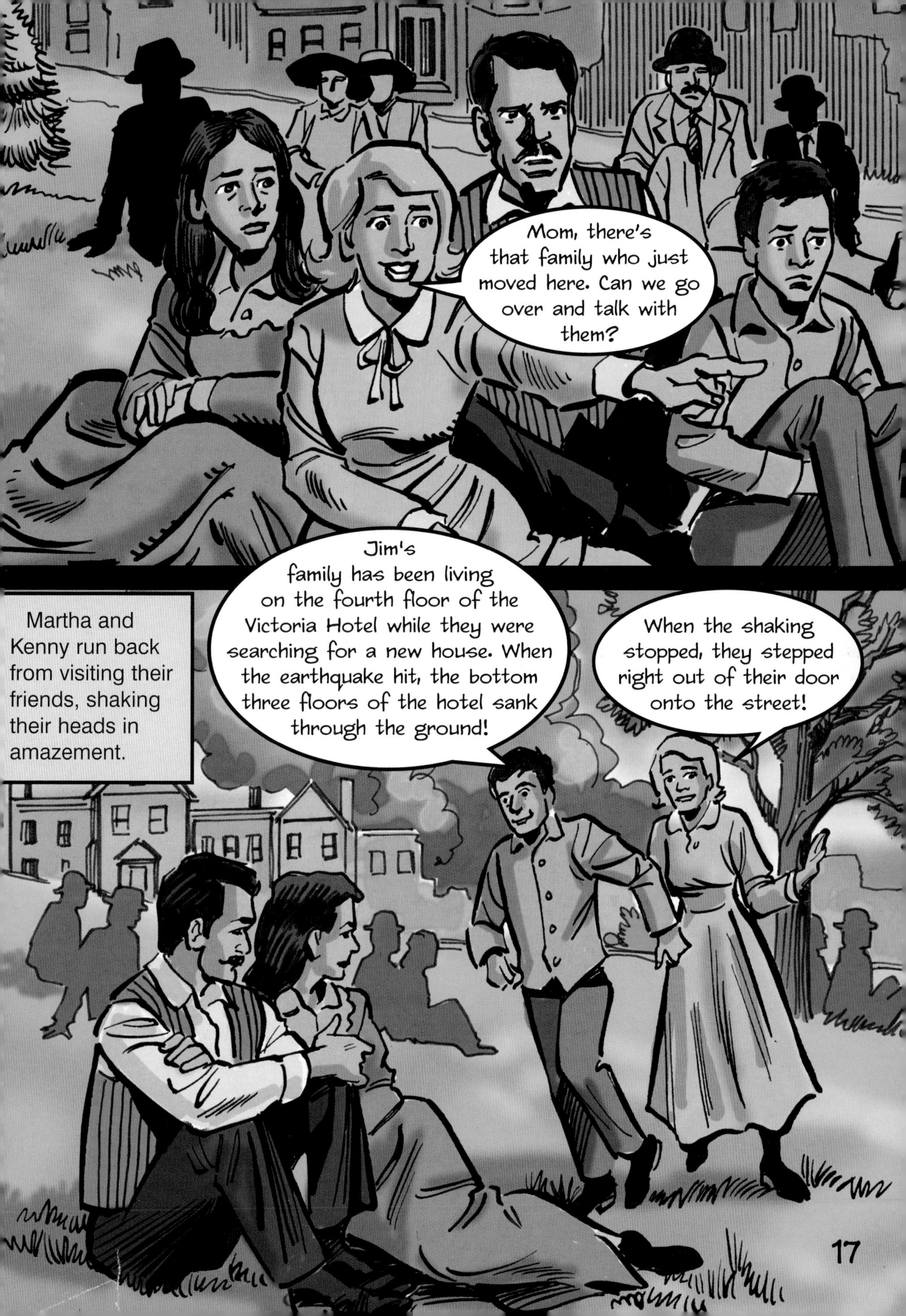
Mom, there's that family who just moved here. Can we go over and talk with them?
Martha and Kenny run back from visiting their friends, shaking their heads in amazement.
Jim's family has been living on the fourth floor of the Victoria Hotel while they were searching for a new house. When the earthquake hit, the bottom three floors of the hotel sank through the ground!
When the shaking stopped, they stepped right out of their door onto the street!

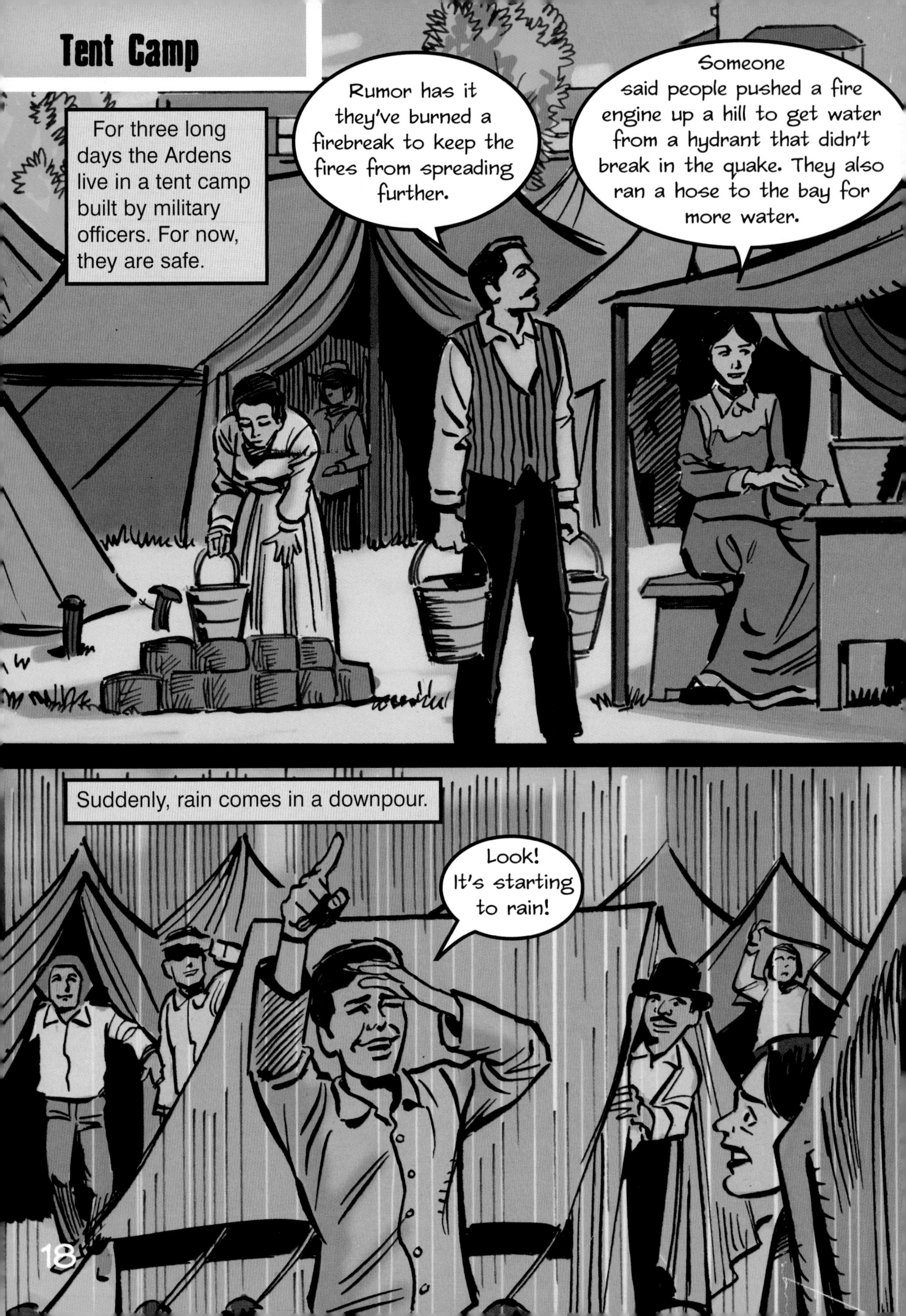
Tent Camp
For three long days the Ardens live in a tent camp built by military officers. For now, they are safe.
Rumor has it they've burned a firebreak to keep the fires from spreading further.
Someone said people pushed a fire engine up a hill to get water from a hydrant that didn't break in the quake. They also ran a hose to the bay for more water.
Suddenly, rain comes in a downpour.
Look! It's starting to rain!

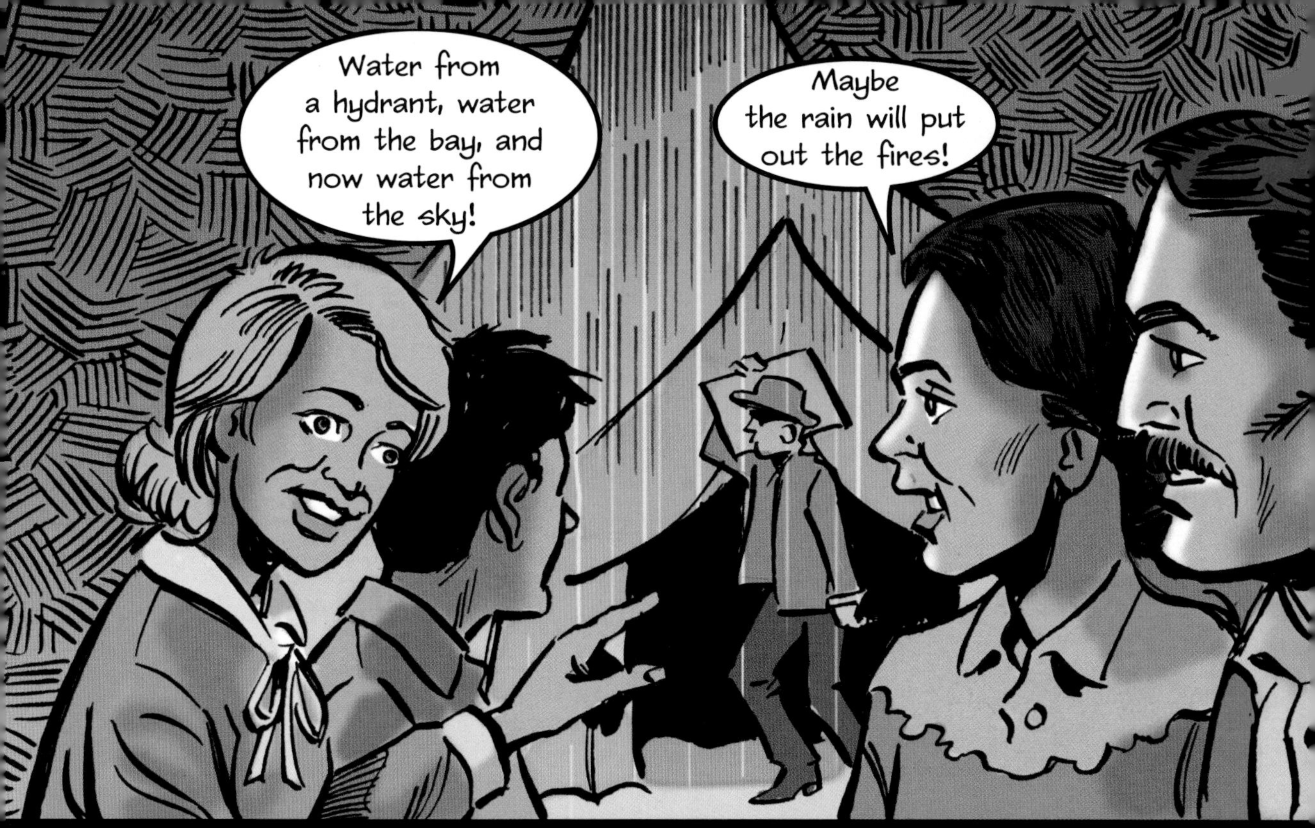
Water from a hydrant, water from the bay, and now water from the sky!
Maybe the rain will put out the fires!

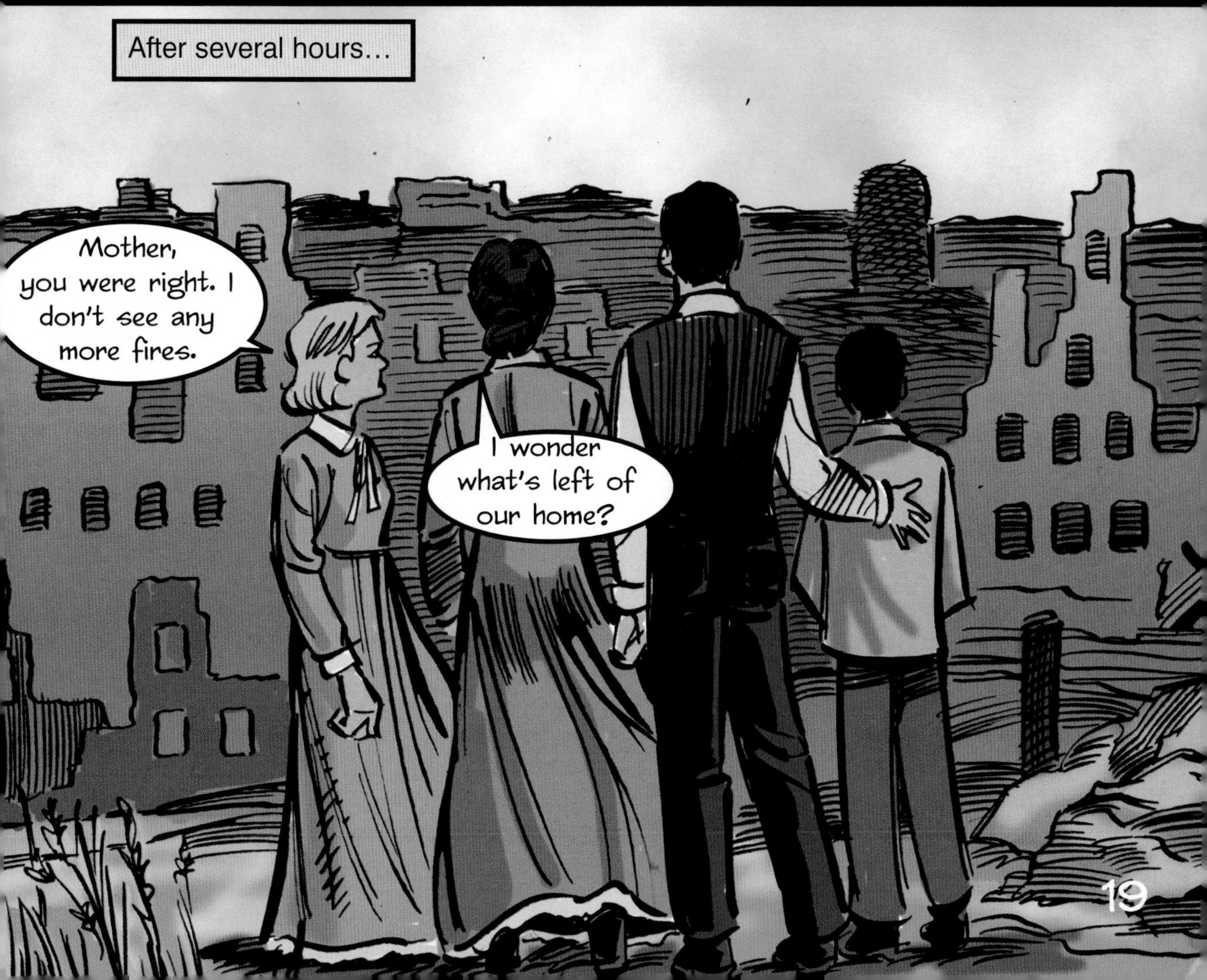
After several hours…
Mother, you were right. I don't see any more fires.
I wonder what's left of our home?

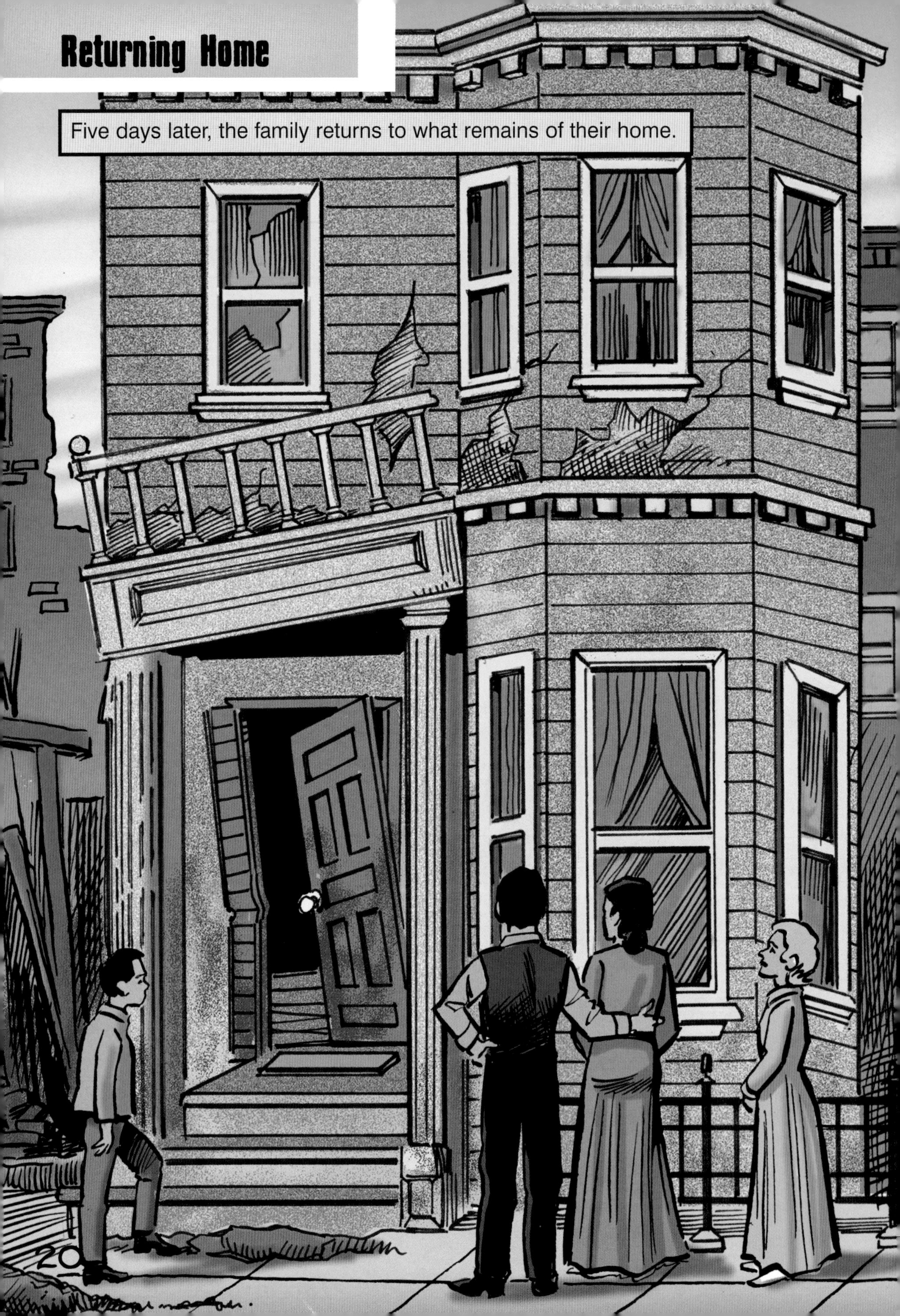
Returning Home
Five days later, the family returns to what remains of their home.

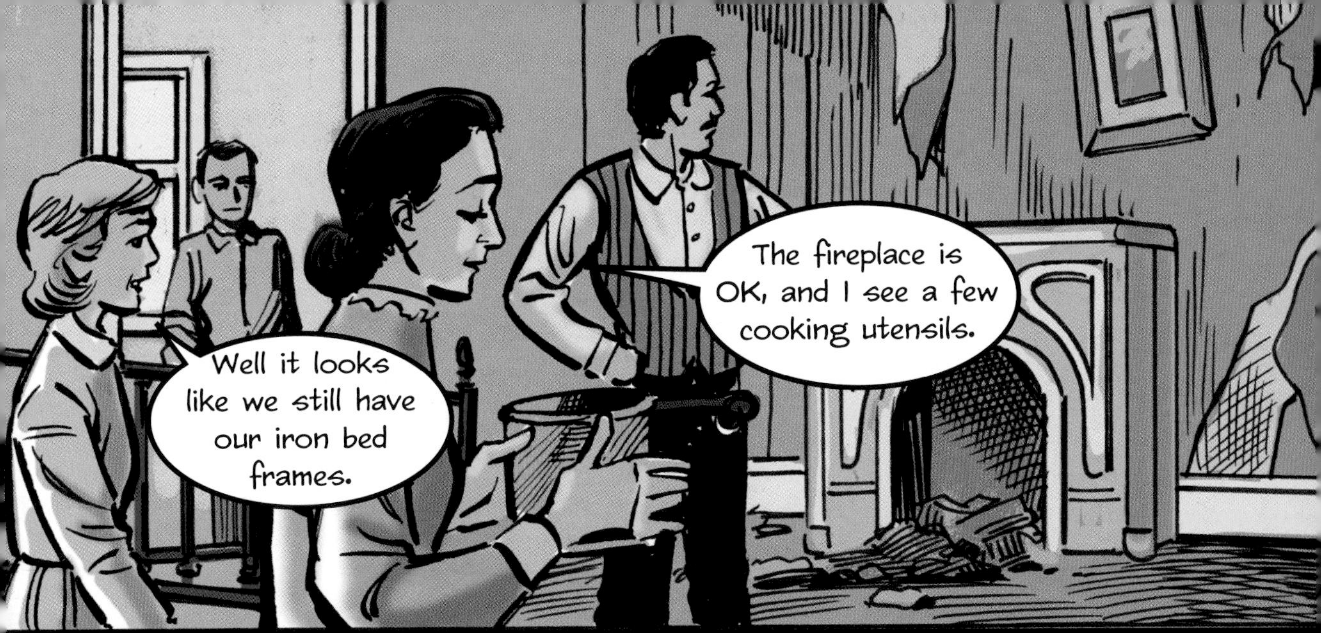
Well it looks like we still have our iron bed frames.
The fireplace is OK, and I see a few cooking utensils.

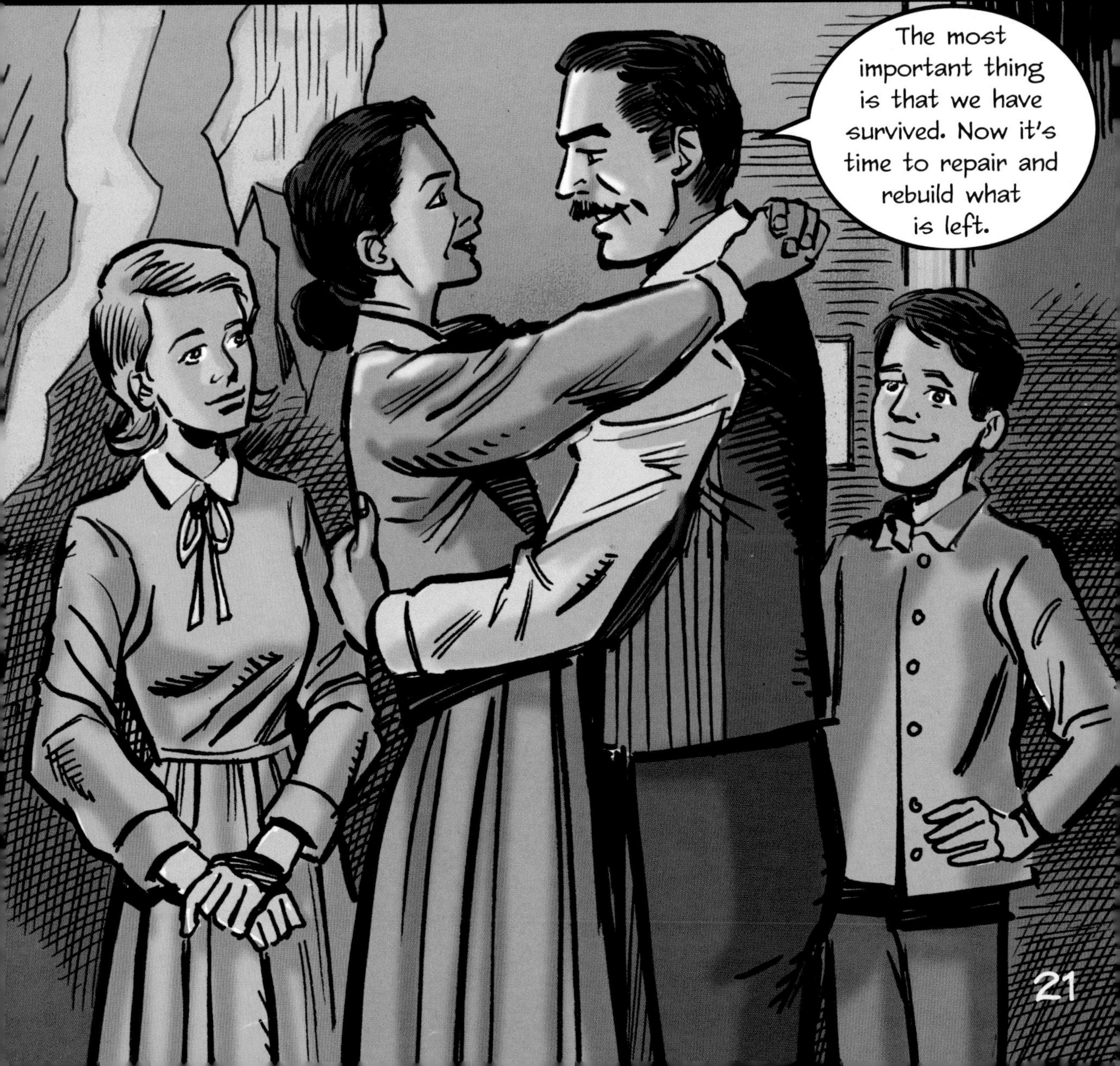
The most important thing is that we have survived. Now it's time to repair and rebuild what is left.

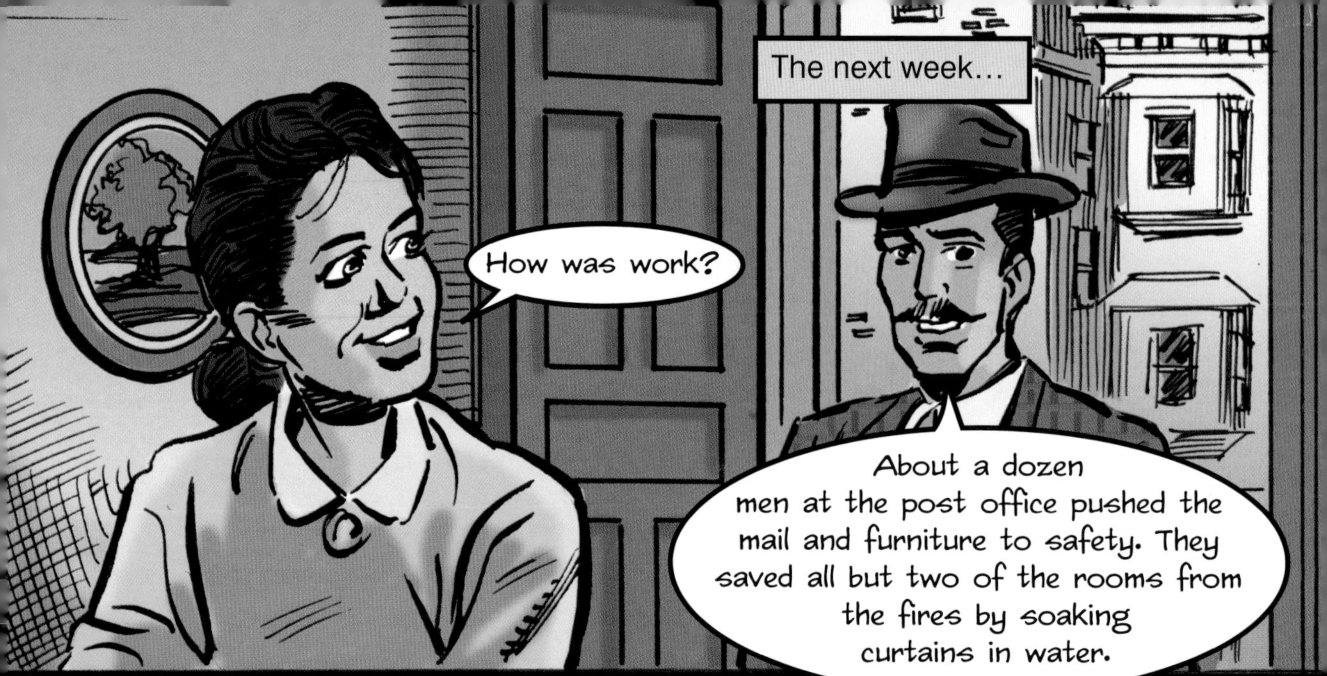
The next week…
How was work?
About a dozen men at the post office pushed the mail and furniture to safety. They saved all but two of the rooms from the fires by soaking curtains in water.

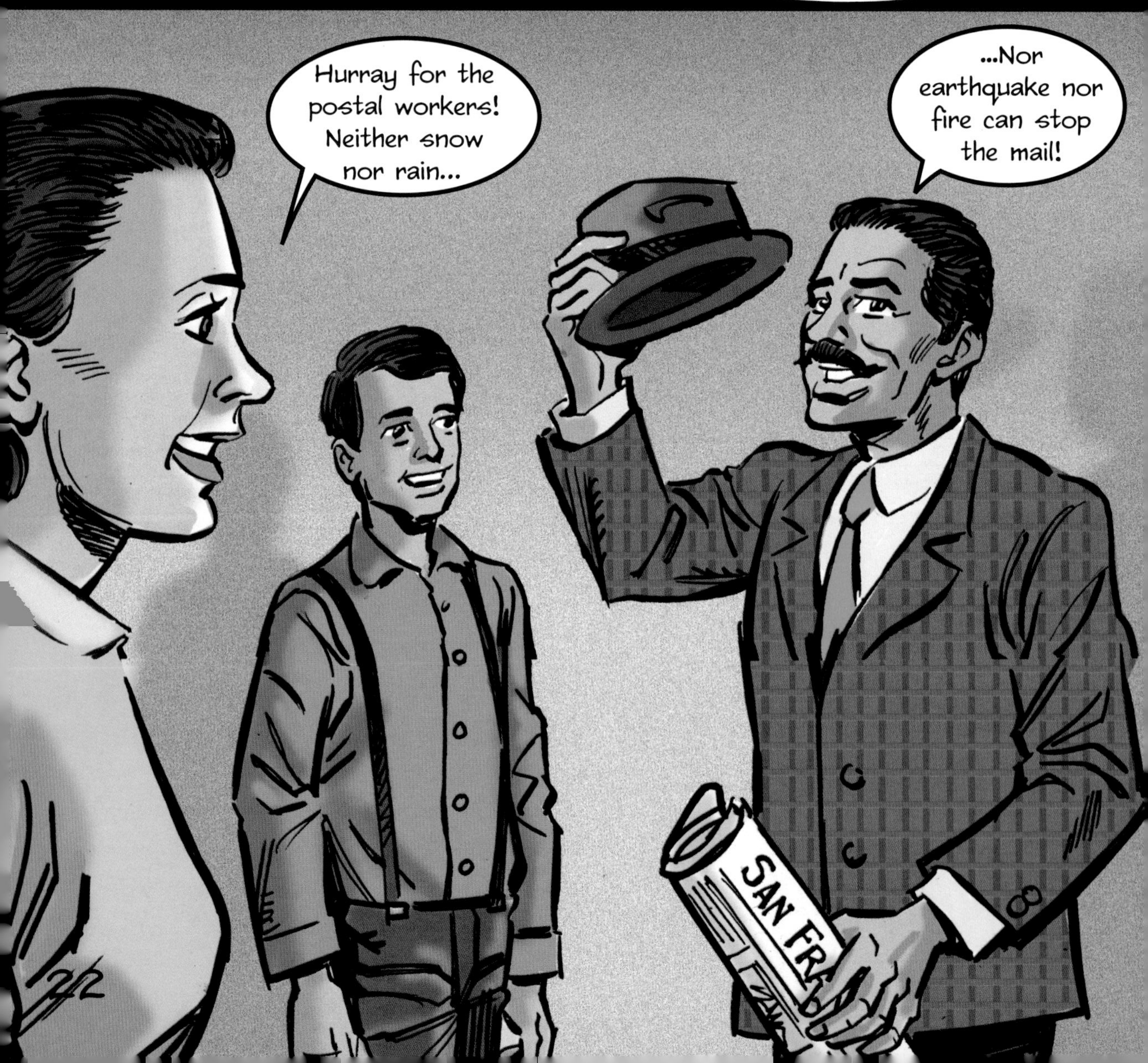
Hurray for the postal workers! Neither snow nor rain...
...Nor earthquake nor fire can stop the mail!
SAN FR

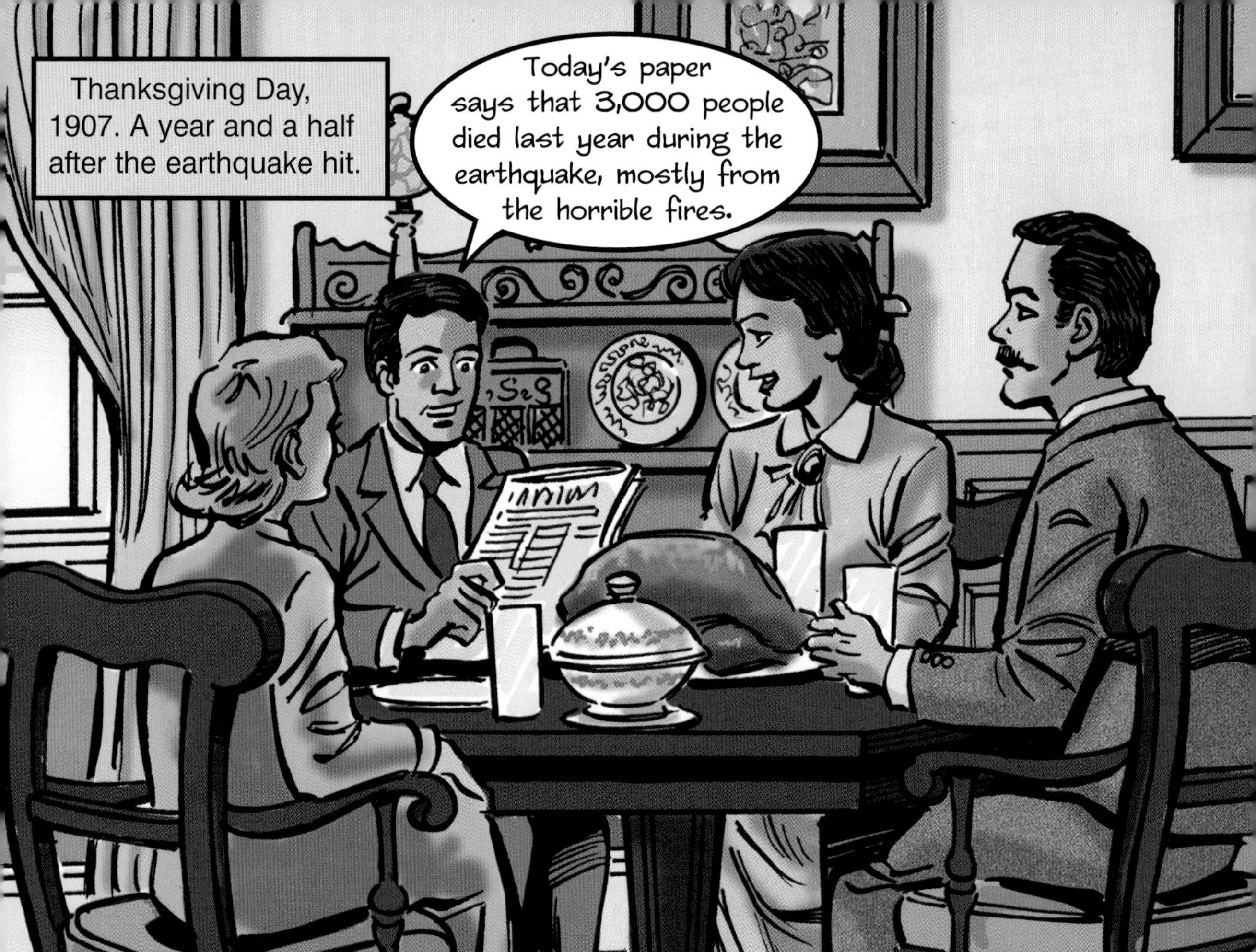
Thanksgiving Day, 1907. A year and a half after the earthquake hit.
Today's paper says that 3,000 people died last year during the earthquake, mostly from the horrible fires.

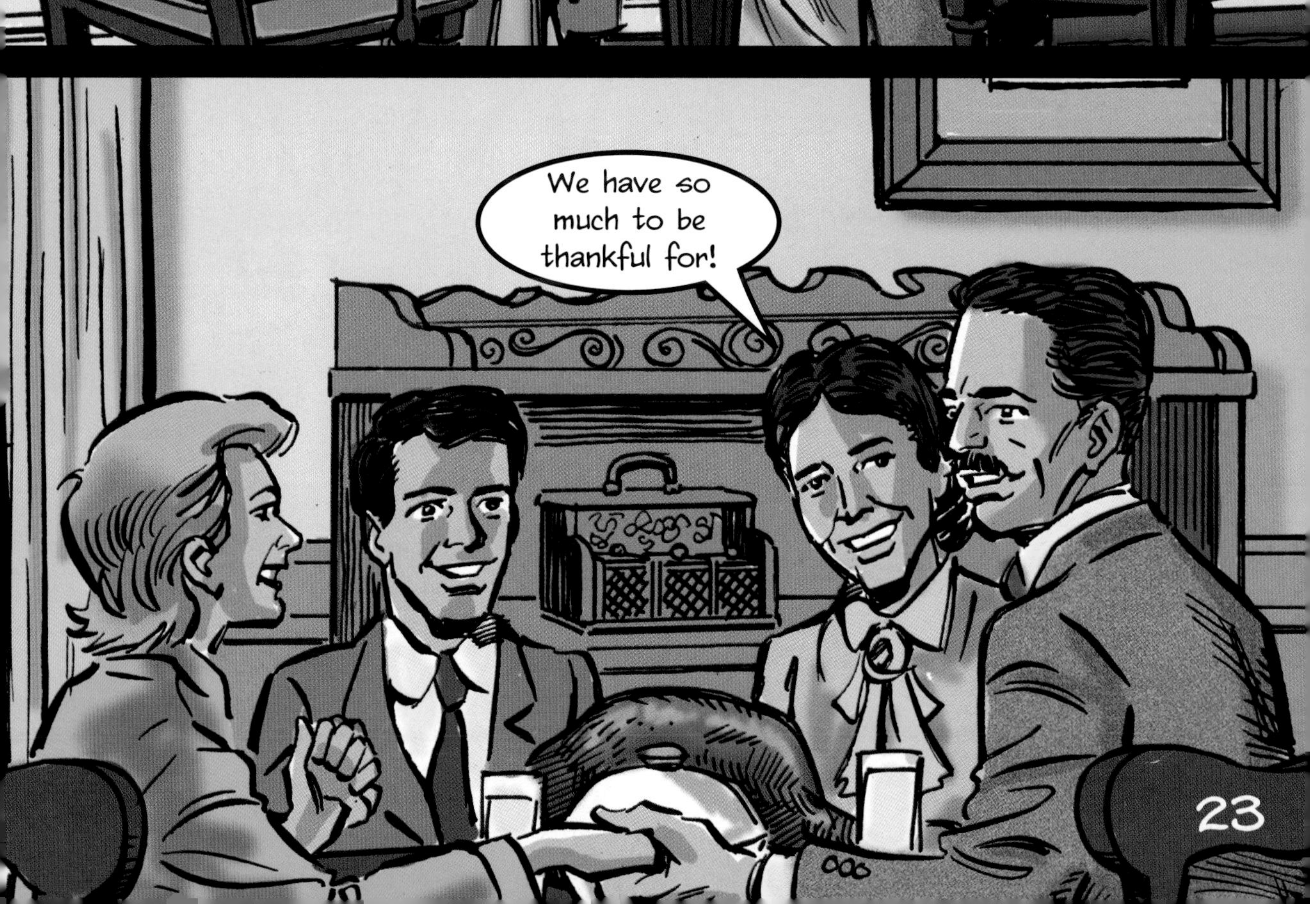
We have so much to be thankful for!

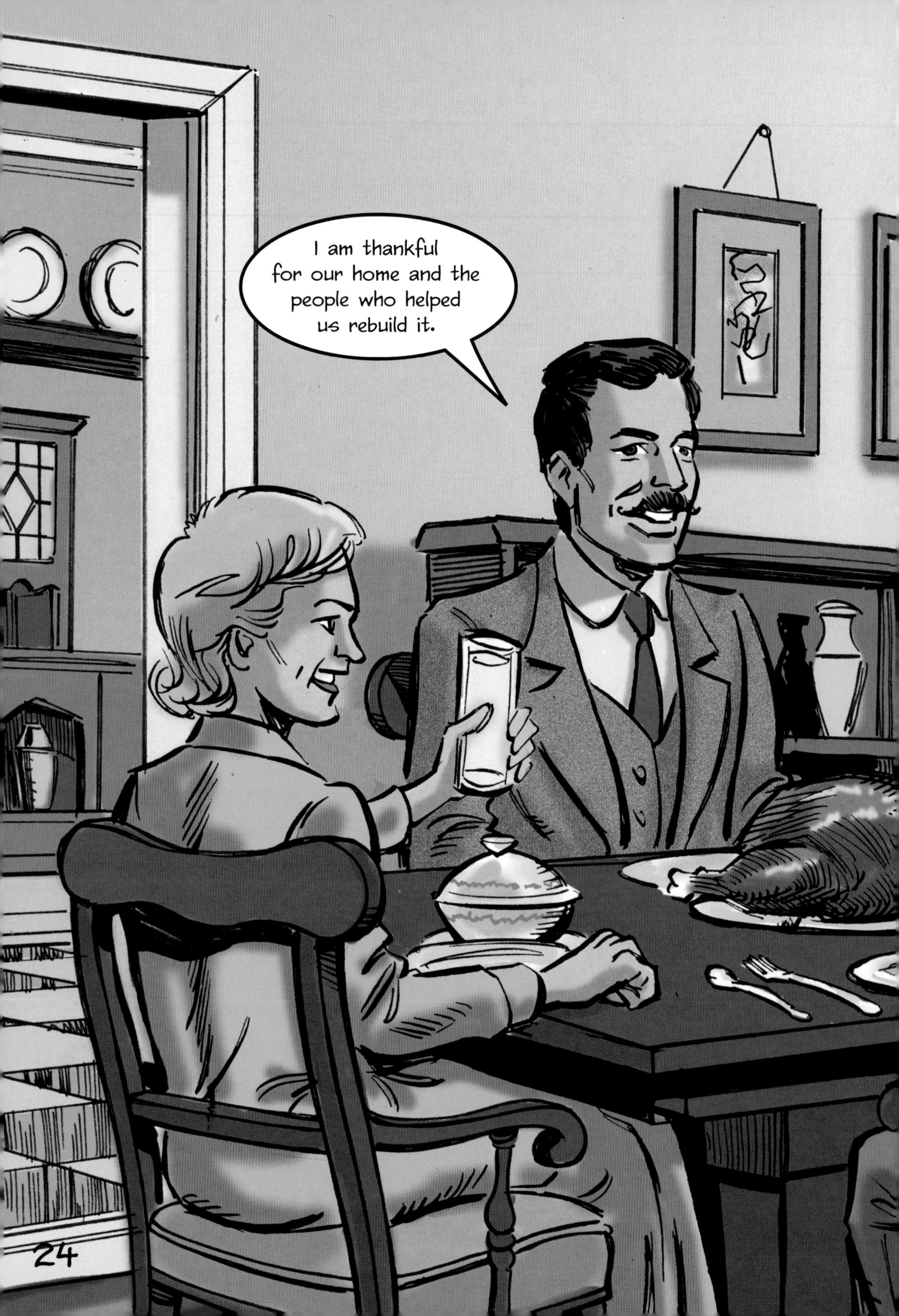
I am thankful for our home and the people who helped us rebuild it.

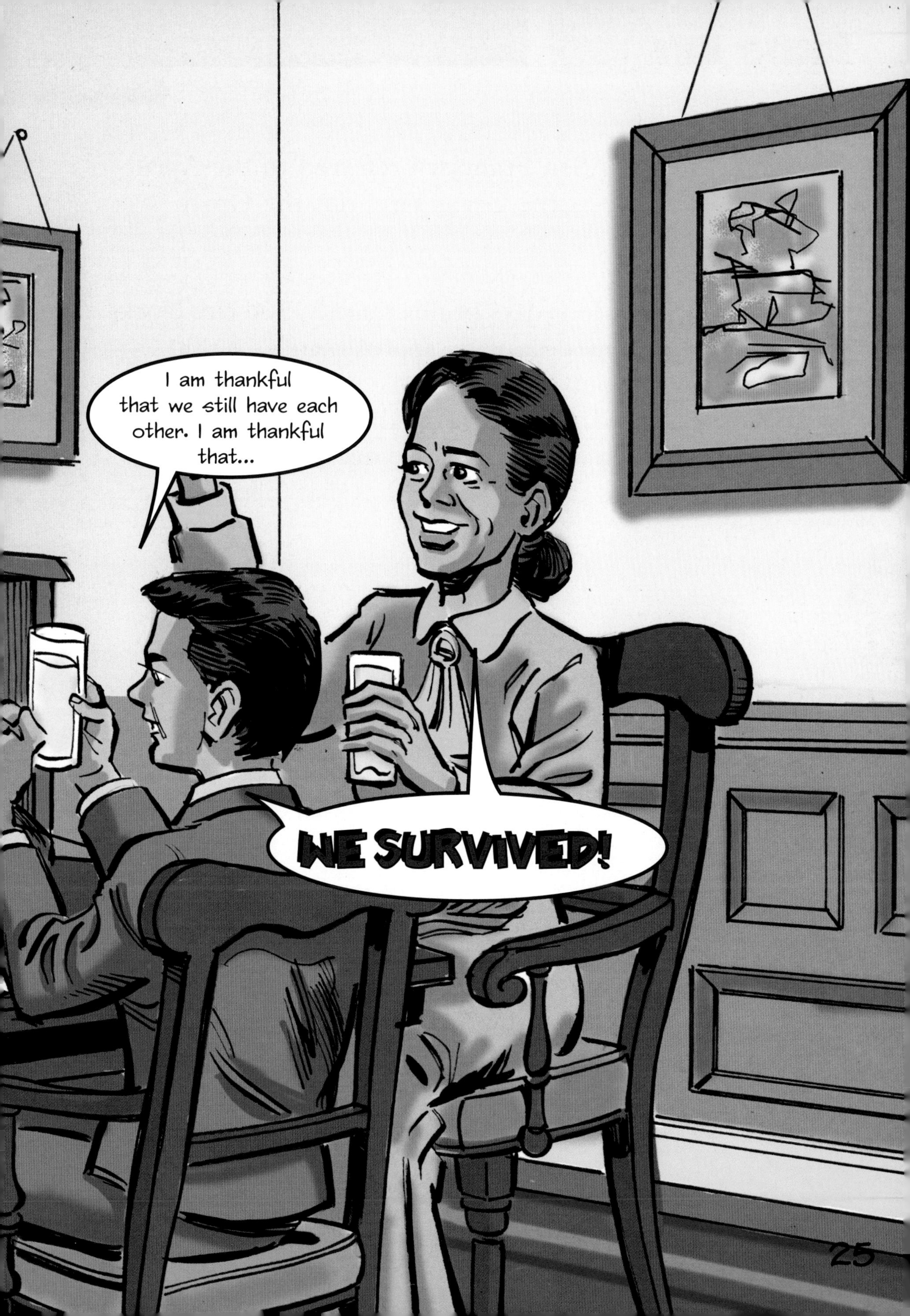
I am thankful that we still have each other. I am thankful that...
WE SURVIVED!

The people of San Francisco referred to the April 1906 disaster as the Great Fire, not the Great Earthquake.

During the four days of this tragedy, 500 city blocks were wiped out, destroying approximately 28,000 buildings. About 225,000 people were left homeless, and 3,000 died. It is estimated that only two percent of this damage was cause by the quaking of the earth. The major loss came from the fires that followed the earthquake.

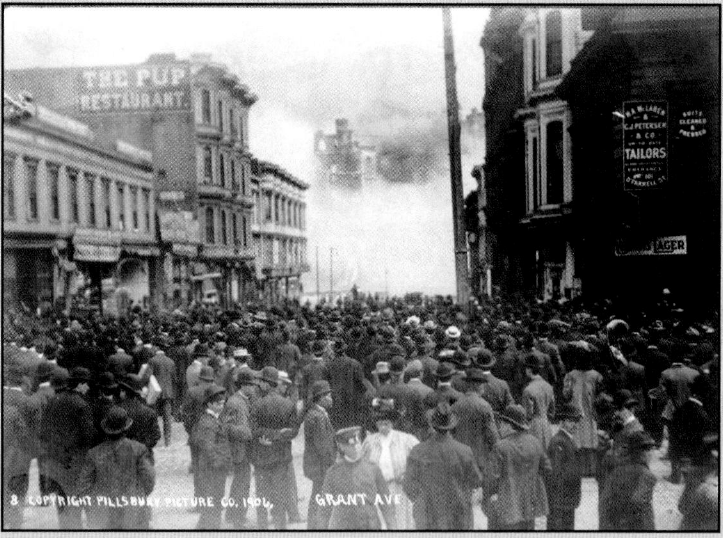
THE PUP
RESTAURANT
TAILORS
8 COPYRIGHT PILLSBURY PICTURE CO. 1906.
GRANT AVE

People gathered together on Grant Avenue in San Francisco and watched as buildings burned out of control.

The San Francisco water system was unprepared for this 1906 emergency.

In 1900, Fire Chief Dennis Sullivan filed reports that the city needed **sprinkler systems** and repairs to the water **cisterns**, some of which were filled with trash. His calls for improvements were ignored. In 1906, Sullivan was sleeping in the fire station when the quake struck. He was killed when the building collapsed with him in it.

The fire wagons had an unusual warning plan.

In 1906, there were no fire trucks with wailing sirens. Instead, the firemen sent barking dogs ahead of them, warning people of approaching hook-and-ladder wagons being pulled by horses. By 1913, fire vehicles had sirens run by a hand crank and ringing bells as a warning system.

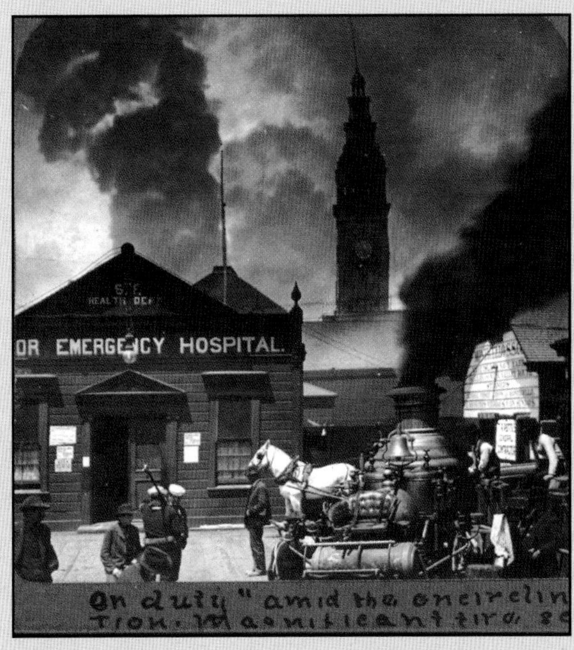
HOSPITAL.

Shortly after 1906, gas-powered vehicles replaced the slower, horse drawn wagons.

Memories Remain

On the morning of the earthquake, a four-year-old boy was slammed against a brick wall, face first. The **impact** broke his nose. That little boy grew up to be one of the most famous of all American photographers, Ansel Adams. His nose remained disfigured for the rest of his life.

At dawn on the fourth day of the disaster, the fire fighters were thrilled to locate one active fire hydrant. This was the source of water that they needed to control the raging fires.

For over 100 years, annual celebrations have been held to **commemorate** that date in history. Each year, the hydrant is repainted gold at the celebration. It stands as a reminder of the role it played in saving the city of San Francisco.

The golden hydrant stands at the corner of Dolores and 20th Street in San Francisco.

Could an earthquake happen where you live?

Earthquakes occur along faults in the Earth's surface. The faults allow the blocks of rock that make up the Earth's surface to move. When two blocks slide past each other quickly, an earthquake occurs.

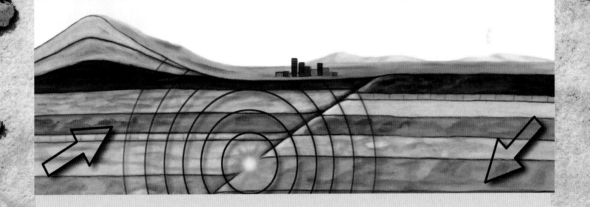

Websites

magma.nationalgeographic.com/ngexplorer/0604/
   articles/mainarticle.html

www.weatherwizkids.com/earthquake1.htm

www.sfmuseum.net/1906/photos.html

www.livescience.com/php/multimedia/imagegallery/
   igviewer.php?gid=44

earthquake.usgs.gov/regional/nca/1906/18april/index.php

Glossary

bay (BAY): A place where ocean water makes an inlet in the land. It is like a pocket of water along the shore.

billows (BIL-ohs): Rises up in large clouds.

cisterns (SISS-turns): Big tanks for holding water.

commemorate (kuh-MEM-uh-rate): To spend time or create a symbol to remember a special person or event.

collapses (kuh-LAPS-is): Falls down. Shifting of the earth, or earthquakes, can cause buildings to collapse.

disaster (duh-ZASS-tur): An event that causes very serious problems.

impact (IM-pakt): When two things run into each other.

makeshift (MAKE-shift): Made quickly to solve a problem for a short time. A makeshift bridge would only be useful for a limited time before it became dangerous.

power outage (POU-ur OUT-ij): An event when electrical lines break and the power is cut off. Nothing plugged into sockets works.

sprinkler systems (SPRINGK-lur SISS-tuhms): Automatic watering devices. Modern buildings have sprinkler systems that spray water when they detect smoke or heat from a fire.

survive (sur-VIVE): To stay alive.

tremor (TREM-ur): Slight shaking of the earth's crust. It is smaller than an earthquake and is usually felt either a distance from an earthquake, or when the earthquake starts to ease up.

Index

City Hall 15
cisterns 27
damage 26
fire(s) 4, 5, 11, 12, 13, 15, 18, 19, 21, 22, 23, 26, 27, 28
fire trucks 27
firemen 27
military 18
policemen 14

earthquake 4, 5, 6, 12, 17, 22, 23, 26, 28
rain 18, 19, 22
tent 18
Victoria Hotel 17
water 12, 13, 18, 19, 22, 27, 28

About the Author

Jo Cleland, Professor Emeritus of Reading Education, taught in the College of Education at Arizona State University for 11 years. Prior to entering university teaching, Jo spent 20 years in public education and continues to work with children through her storytelling and workshops. She has presented to audiences of teachers and students across the nation and the world, bringing to all her favorite message: **what we learn with delight, we never forget**.

About the Illustrator

Pete McDonnell is an illustrator who has worked worked in his field for 24 years. He has been creating comics, storyboards, and pop-art style illustrations for clients such as Marvel Comics, the History Channel, Microsoft, Nestle, Sega, and many more. He lives in Sonoma County, California with his wife Shannon (also an illustrator) and son Jacob.